Ron Stewart

A Field Guide to the
FLAMING GORGE-UINTAS
National Scenic Byway

by
Mary Beth Bennis-Smith,
Utah Field House of Natural History State Park Museum
Douglas A. Sprinkel,
Utah Geological Survey
Ron Stewart,
Utah Division of Wildlife Resources
Linda West
Tom Elder
Nancy Bostick-Ebbert

"WILDLIFE THROUGH THE AGES"

The Donning Company Publishers
184 Business Park Drive, Suite 206
Virginia Beach, VA 23462

Steve Mull, General Manager
Barbara Buchanan, Office Manager
Heather Floyd, Editor
Scott Rule, Graphic Designer
Derek Eley, Imaging Artist
Debby Dowell, Project Research Coordinator
Scott Rule, Director of Marketing
Tonya Hannink, Marketing Coordinator

Ed Williams, Project Director

Library of Congress Cataloging-in-Publication Data

A field guide to the Flaming Gorge-Uintas National Scenic Byway / by Mary Beth Bennis-Smith ... [et al.].
    p. cm.
 Includes bibliographical references and index.
 ISBN-13: 978-1-57864-488-9 (softcover : alk. paper)
 1. Flaming Gorge-Uintas Scenic Byway (Utah)--Guidebooks. I. Bennis-Smith, Mary Beth, 1963-
 F832.F52F54 2008
 917.92'1502--dc22
                          2008004651

Printed in the United States of America at Walsworth Publishing Company

This Book is Dedicated to:

Terry W. Smith
1963–2005

Beloved husband, esteemed friend and colleague, a man who dedicated his life to protecting the resources of this area.

Ed Johnson/Courtesy UDWR

TABLE OF CONTENTS

ACKNOWLEDGMENTS

The authors would like to thank the following people for their technical expertise and/or editorial review of the manuscript:

Dan Abeyta, Larry Cesspooch, Gayle DeCamp, Heather Finlayson, Sherel Goodrich, Michael D. Hylland, Bryon Loosle, Clint McKnight, Diane Probasco, Heather Shilton, Andy Simpson, Steve Sroka, and Grant C. Willis.

With gratitude, we remember the following agencies for their support of time, resources, and/or funding of this project:

Ashley National Forest, Chevron Corporation, Flaming Gorge-Uintas Scenic Byway Committee, FHA National Scenic Byways Program, Intermountain Natural History Association, Uintah Impact Mitigation Special Service District, Utah Field House of Natural History, Utah Geological Survey, Utah State Parks, and Utah Division of Wildlife Resources.

For the inspiration they provided, we acknowledge:

Luke Duncan, Tom Freestone, Shirley Murdock Reed, and Chalmers Wash.

Ron Stewart

INTRODUCTION

Scenic byways might be described as the crown jewels of our road and highway systems. Designated by the U.S. Secretary of Transportation, each byway has one or more outstanding features that secure its position in this elite designation. The byway may possess archaeological, historical, scenic, cultural, recreational, or natural significance. Although designated for its "Wildlife Through the Ages" theme, the Flaming Gorge-Uintas National Scenic Byway satisfies many of the qualifying criteria. Scenic byways provide Americans, and visitors from abroad, the opportunity to view America at its best.

The Flaming Gorge-Uintas National Scenic Byway was designated in 1998. Scenic vistas, deep canyons, geologic wonders, wildlife viewing, and various recreational opportunities abound along the Byway. As you wind your way up and over the eastern Uinta Mountains, almost one billion years of Earth's history is exposed, from the Precambrian, when life was in its infancy, through the Miocene Epoch, when prehistoric mammals roamed. Geologists call these layered rocks "formations." Each formation is a record of an extinct ecosystem, characterized by certain types of rock and often having a unique assemblage of plant and animal remains. The nineteenth-century paleontologist Joseph Leidy, as he contemplated these ideas, wrote:

"When I thought of the buttes beneath my feet, with their entombed remains of multitudes of animals forever extinct… I truly felt that I was standing on the wreck of a former world."

Study the various plant communities during the drive and the associated wildlife that occurs within each. Even after a short time, it becomes clear that these communities are intimately tied to the geology, which plays a deciding factor in the "where" and "how" of their existence. Consider then the dominion that geology holds over human civilizations. The basic survival questions asked by all cultures, such as where to find food, water, and shelter, have their answers firmly rooted in the geology of any given area.

As you drive this Byway, challenge yourself to look beyond the magnificence of the view. Consider you are, in essence, looking at both the past and the present of Earth's story—and potentially the future, based on the stewardship these areas receive. Today we make the choices that will either ensure the protection of areas such as these or destroy them through indifference or poor decisions. What and how we decide will be reflective of our stewardship philosophies. Do we believe the Earth was given to us by our parents, or borrowed from our children?

A Billion Years in the Making

Geology and Paleontology of the Byway

Douglas A. Sprinkel and Mary Beth Bennis-Smith

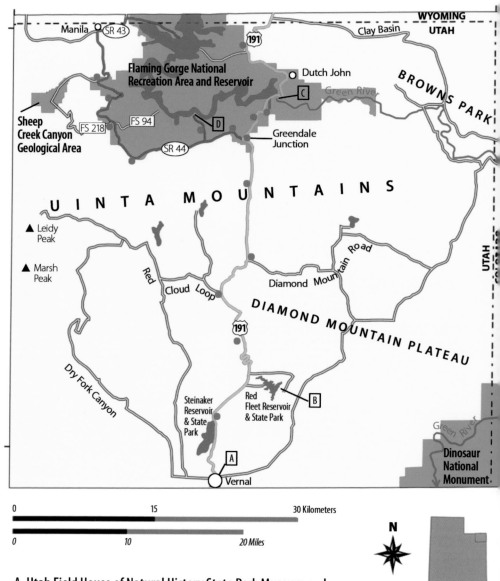

0   15   30 Kilometers

0   10   20 Miles

N

A. Utah Field House of Natural History State Park Museum and Information Center

B. Dinosaur Trackway Trail

C. Flaming Gorge Dam and Visitor Center

D. Red Canyon Overlook and Visitor Center

● Byway Interpretive Sites

What makes the Flaming Gorge-Uintas National Scenic Byway such a spectacular drive? It is the combination of the expansive landscape and the plant and animal communities. Underlying it all is the geology! The geology dictates how the landscape takes shape and to a large degree where plants and animals (and humans!) live. The variety of geologic formations exposed along the route reveal nearly 1 billion years of Earth's history. Thirty formations comprising about 36,000 feet—almost seven miles—of rock preserve evidence of past environments ranging from warm shallow seas to ancient coastlines and Sahara-like sand dune fields. Locked in the rock are the fossil remains of plant and animal communities that lived millions of years ago. Some are extinct but many have modern descendants.

In general, the youngest formations are exposed as east-to-west bands along the north and south flanks of the Uinta Mountains. As you drive into and ascend the Uintas, the exposed formations get progressively older until you reach the Precambrian Uinta Mountain Group in the core of the range. Then, the formations are repeated, becoming younger as you descend the other side into the adjoining basin. The formations are laid out in this manner because the Uinta Mountains were elevated along faults and folded into a broad arch about 70 to 35 million years ago during a regional mountain-building event called the Laramide orogeny. Concurrent and subsequent erosion methodically cut into and removed the overlying Mesozoic and Paleozoic rocks from the crest of the Uintas, exposing the oldest rocks in their core and the younger rocks along the edges.

GEOLOGIC HISTORY

About 1 billion years of geologic history unfolds along the Flaming Gorge-Uintas National Scenic Byway, and an additional 2 billion years of the Earth's past is revealed in the surrounding area. Travel along the Scenic Byway reveals a rich history of shallow oceans teeming with life, ancient river systems, vast sand dune fields, and an extensive lake.

PRECAMBRIAN

We will start at the beginning. East of the Scenic Byway, in the mountains north of Browns Park, some of the oldest rocks in Utah are exposed. We start there because similar rocks of the Paleoproterozoic Red Creek Quartzite likely underlie the Uinta Mountain Group along the Byway. The early history of these rocks is uncertain, but most geologists believe that marine sediments, which would eventually become the Red Creek Quartzite, accumulated offshore from what was the edge of ancient North America (Archean-age Wyoming province). These rocks were buried and subjected to

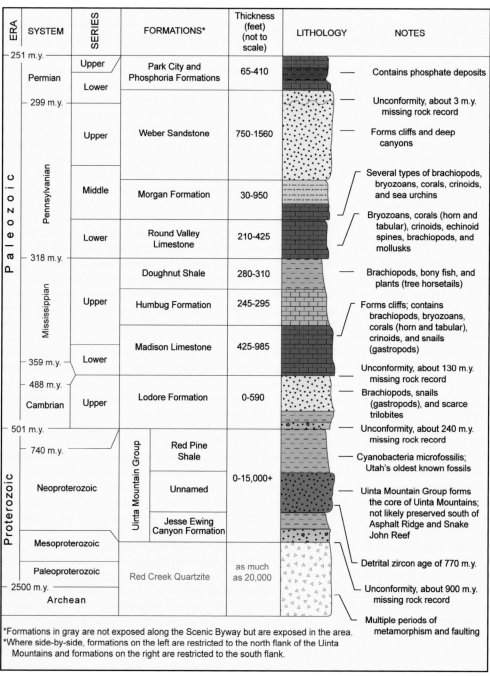

ERA	SYSTEM	SERIES	FORMATIONS*	Thickness (feet) (not to scale)	LITHOLOGY	NOTES
Paleozoic — 251 m.y.	Permian	Upper	Park City and Phosphoria Formations	65-410		Contains phosphate deposits
	— 299 m.y.	Lower				Unconformity, about 3 m.y. missing rock record
	Pennsylvanian	Upper	Weber Sandstone	750-1560		Forms cliffs and deep canyons
		Middle	Morgan Formation	30-950		Several types of brachiopods, bryozoans, corals, crinoids, and sea urchins
		Lower	Round Valley Limestone	210-425		Bryozoans, corals (horn and tabular), crinoids, echinoid spines, brachiopods, and mollusks
	— 318 m.y. Mississippian	Upper	Doughnut Shale	280-310		Brachiopods, bony fish, and plants (tree horsetails)
			Humbug Formation	245-295		Forms cliffs; contains brachiopods, bryozoans, corals (horn and tabular), crinoids, and snails (gastropods)
		Lower	Madison Limestone	425-985		
	— 359 m.y. — 488 m.y. Cambrian	Upper	Lodore Formation	0-590		Unconformity, about 130 m.y. missing rock record; Brachiopods, snails (gastropods), and scarce trilobites
Proterozoic — 501 m.y. — 740 m.y. Neoproterozoic		Uinta Mountain Group	Red Pine Shale	0-15,000+		Unconformity, about 240 m.y. missing rock record; Cyanobacteria microfossilis; Utah's oldest known fossils
			Unnamed			Uinta Mountain Group forms the core of Uinta Mountains; not likely preserved south of Asphalt Ridge and Snake John Reef
	Mesoproterozoic		Jesse Ewing Canyon Formation			Detrital zircon age of 770 m.y.
	Paleoproterozoic — 2500 m.y. Archean		Red Creek Quartzite	as much as 20,000		Unconformity, about 900 m.y. missing rock record; Multiple periods of metamorphism and faulting

*Formations in gray are not exposed along the Scenic Byway but are exposed in the area.
*Where side-by-side, formations on the left are restricted to the north flank of the Uinta Mountains and formations on the right are restricted to the south flank.

Doug Sprinkel

multiple periods of faulting, folding, and high-grade metamorphism between 2.7 and 2.5 billion years ago. The Red Creek Quartzite was deformed again during a period that began about 2.4 billion years ago and spanned about 700 million years. About 1.7 billion years ago, regional compression, or squeezing, caused by Paleoproterozoic continental collision along a geologic feature called the Cheyenne suture zone welded the Red Creek Quartzite against the older Archean crust of the Wyoming province and enlarged the continent. Subsequent block faulting uplifted the Red Creek Quartzite as much as 23,000 feet. Erosion reduced the Red Creek highlands to rolling hills prior to deposition of the Uinta Mountain Group.

Downward movement on the south side (in today's direction) of the Cheyenne suture zone fault system about 800 million years ago created a basin in which non-marine to marine rocks (sandstone, shale, and conglomerate) of the Neoproterozoic Uinta Mountain Group accumulated. By the time deposition ended about 740 million years ago, as much as 15,000 feet (and possibly as much as 20,000 feet) of rock had been deposited. Uplift followed deposition, which tilted and eroded the Uinta Mountain Group before deposition of the Cambrian Lodore Formation about 500 million years ago.

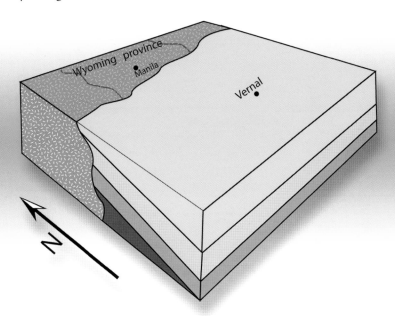

More than 2.5 billion years ago, the area that would become the Uinta Mountains was near the shore of an ancient sea. The sediments deposited on the seabed would become sandstone, limestone, and shale. Continued burial, heat, and pressure metamorphosed the sedimentary rocks into the quartzite, marble, and schist of the Red Creek Quartzite.

Deep though it is, Red Canyon exposes only a small part of the Uinta Mountain Group's great thickness of layered rock.

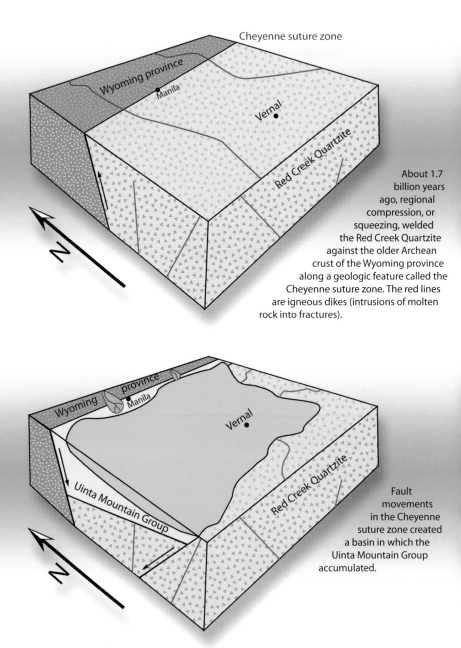

Cheyenne suture zone

Wyoming province

Manila

Vernal

Red Creek Quartzite

N

About 1.7 billion years ago, regional compression, or squeezing, welded the Red Creek Quartzite against the older Archean crust of the Wyoming province along a geologic feature called the Cheyenne suture zone. The red lines are igneous dikes (intrusions of molten rock into fractures).

Wyoming province

Manila

Vernal

Uinta Mountain Group

Red Creek Quartzite

N

Fault movements in the Cheyenne suture zone created a basin in which the Uinta Mountain Group accumulated.

FLUCTUATING PALEOZOIC SEAS

The Lodore Formation (and correlative formations) records an influx of the Cambrian sea that flooded much of the region. Its thickness varies from zero to as much as 590 feet because the sea flooded an irregular surface that developed during

Oldest Life in Utah

Although not the largest fossils found along the Byway, without question some of the most important are the microscopic cyanobacteria collected from the Uinta Mountain Group. Cyanobacteria are among the oldest fossils on Earth, dating back about 3.5 billion years into the Archean, and are thought to be largely responsible for supplying the oxygen to Earth's early atmosphere. Samples collected along the Byway are thought to have lived about 800 million years ago in the middle Neoproterozoic, making them the oldest known fossils in Utah.

Perhaps even more amazing than their longevity within the fossil record are the processes of evolution that we find documented in the fossils themselves. The oldest samples show non-colonial organisms with simple cell walls. However, slightly higher up, and therefore younger in age, samples are characterized by more complex cell walls and the formation of colonies.

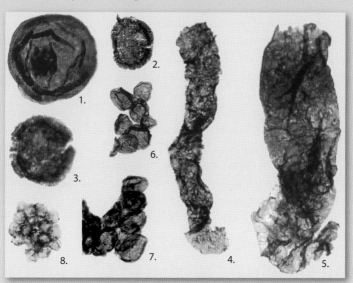

Representative microfossils from the Uinta Mountain Group, eastern Uinta Mountains.
1. *Leiosphaeridia spp.*, unnamed formation   2. *Satka sp.*, unnamed formation
3. *Trachysphaeridium laminaritum*, unnamed formation   4–5. algal filament fragments, unnamed formation   6–7. *Eosaccharomyces sp.*, unnamed formation
8. *Eohyella spp.*, Red Pine Shale.

Photomicrographs by Gerald Waanders, from Sprinkel, D. A., and Waanders, G., 2005, "Stratigraphy, Organic Microfossils, and Thermal Maturation of the Neoproterozoic Uinta Mountain Group in the Eastern Uinta Mountains, Northeastern Utah," in Dehler, C. M., Pederson, J. L., Sprinkel, D. A., and Kowallis, B. J., eds., *Uinta Mountain Geology*: Utah Geological Association Publication 33, p. 63–73.

late Neoproterozoic time from about 740 to 500 million years ago. Beginning about 488 million years ago, the Scenic Byway area was at or just above sea level after deposition of the Lodore Formation; there is no record of Ordovician through Devonian rocks, and any sediments that were deposited and lithified (turned into rock) during that time were removed by erosion before the region subsided and sediment accumulation resumed. Mississippian-age seas substantially flooded the region beginning about 359 million years ago.

Sea level fluctuated throughout the remaining Paleozoic time and created two shallowing-upward successions of rock. The first succession includes the Mississippian Madison, Humbug, and Doughnut Formations (about 359 to 318 million years ago). The shallow tropical sea of the Madison Limestone was ideal for carbonate deposition, and animals such as brachiopods, crinoids, and corals flourished. As the seas became shallower, the Humbug Formation and Doughnut Shale were deposited closer to shore; there was even a time when rocks from the Doughnut were deposited within a coastal marsh environment.

The second shallowing-upward succession includes the Pennsylvanian Round Valley, Morgan, and Weber Formations (about 318 to 275 million years ago). The seas again deepened during Round Valley Limestone time in which limestone deposition resumed and marine life flourished. As before, sea level dropped during deposition of the Morgan Formation, but this time the seas withdrew from the region and coastal sand dune fields prevailed as the Weber Sandstone was deposited. The end of the Paleozoic (beginning about 275 to 270 million years ago) saw the return of shallow marine conditions with deposition of the Lower Permian Park City Formation.

Sea level significantly dropped worldwide in the latter part of the Permian. Consequently, Upper Permian rocks are not preserved in the Uinta Mountains, as well as in much of Utah. In addition, an unconformity (a gap in the geologic record) separates Lower Permian rocks from the overlying Lower Triassic rocks, and represents about 21 million years of missing time.

MESOZOIC MARINE–CONTINENTAL TRANSITION

The area crossed by the Scenic Byway remained at or near sea level during much of the Mesozoic Era (about 251 to 65 million years ago), a time of alternating marine and continental deposition. Early Triassic time began with marine deposition of the Dinwoody Formation. That gave way to a mostly nonmarine environment that was dominated by broad river (fluvial) flood plains of the Moenkopi Formation. Triassic time also heralded the appearance of early dinosaurs in the region. A 15-million-year hiatus separates the Moenkopi and overlying Chinle Formation. The basal Chinle Formation—Gartra Member—signaled a return of fluvial deposition. The Gartra

Sea Shells in Utah

Brachiopods are modern invertebrates that first appeared in the fossil record in Early Cambrian time, approximately 530 million years ago. This strictly marine group is not related to the bivalves (oysters and clams), although certain similarities exist. Because of their rapid and diverse evolution, brachiopods may be used as index fossils, useful in providing the relative age of a rock unit.

Spirifer increbescens from the Madison Limestone.
FHPR specimen 831/Courtesy UFH

Extinct and Extant

We learn about the past by studying the present. One such example is corals, an ancient lineage of animals dating back 515 million years ago through present day. Studies of living corals help us to interpret extinct corals, which in turn give clues to past oceanic conditions such as depth, salinity, and temperature.

Horn corals are now extinct, but were common in the Pennsylvanian Period. Above: FHPR specimen 1135/ Courtesy UFH Right: FHPR specimen 2359/Linda West

The Pennsylvanian–Permian Weber Sandstone commonly forms steep, rugged cliffs where exposed in the eastern Uinta Mountains. The Weber, like the Nugget Sandstone, consists of ancient sand dune deposits. View southwest along U.S. 191 north of the phosphate mine.
Ron Stewart/Courtesy UDWR

consists of coarse fluvial-channel deposits that are deeply incised into the underlying Moenkopi Formation. This formation typically contains petrified wood.

The uppermost part of the Chinle Formation records the first signs of the sea of sand that eventually would become the great sand dune desert preserved in the Upper Triassic–Lower Jurassic Nugget Sandstone (Wingate Sandstone and Navajo

Bedding dip combines with erosion of the Triassic Chinle and Triassic–Jurassic Nugget Sandstone to form a series of buttes that resemble battleships plying the open sea. The bow and deck of the ships are the upper Chinle Formation (which may be renamed the Bell Springs Formation), and the ships' superstructure is the Nugget Sandstone. View east from the road to the Dinosaur Trackway Trail east of U.S. 191.
Doug Sprinkel

Windows on the Ancient World

Paleontology, the study of ancient life, attempts to answer numerous and oftentimes very complex questions, not the least of which is how past and present-day life are related. Paleontologists seek the answers to these complex questions through the study of fossils. Arising from the Latin word *fossus* (loosely meaning "dug up"), a fossil is evidence of past life.

Fossilization is a blanket term comprising different processes that preserve the remains of plants and animals in the rock record. Many of these processes are chemical in nature and involve the replacement of organic material with different invasive minerals. One such process is petrification, in which the original organism is totally replaced by minerals. Preservation is generally precise enough that the details of the structure are maintained.

There are laws governing the collection, possession, sale, and/or trade of fossils on public lands. These laws vary depending on the jurisdiction of the land where the fossils occur or were collected. Please check with the appropriate land agency with regard to the law before collecting any fossil. On private ground, fossils are the property of the landowner and cannot be collected without their permission.

Petrified wood from the Chinle Formation.
FHPR specimen 7037/Linda West

Sandstone of southern Utah). Conditions similar to the modern Sahara existed for about 25 million years and deposited more than 900 feet of sand before the ocean once again flooded the region.

The Carmel Formation represents a time of shallow-marine to tidal-flat deposition. Clams, crinoids, and ooliths (small, round accretions of carbonate material) are preserved within the lower limestone beds, indicating shallow-marine conditions. Gypsum and fine-grained sand, silt, and shale—along with sedimentary features—indicate that tidal-flat conditions prevailed during much of the latter part of Carmel time. The Middle Jurassic Carmel sea continued to retreat and dust blew from the newly exposed seabed and dried tidal-flat areas; sand dunes once again drifted across the region and deposited the Entrada Sandstone.

The conspicuous layering preserved in the Triassic–Jurassic Nugget Sandstone is a classic example of cross-beds. Cross-beds can form in several sedimentary environments, but these large-scale cross-beds are typical of multiple cycles of ancient migrating sand dunes. The Nugget Sandstone is correlative in part with the Navajo Sandstone of southern Utah.
Linda West

Walking Across Time

Tracks, such as *Eubrontes* and *Grallator*, are known as trace fossils. A trace fossil is anything an animal leaves behind in the rock record, such as footprints, dung, or burrows. Trackways (sequences of footprints made by one or more animals) provide a unique perspective on extinct life by showing animals in motion, and provide clues to their size, behavior, and/or social structure. An example of this comes from a site in Colorado showing several large *Brontosaurus*-type tracks moving parallel to each other, indicative of herd behavior.

Visit the dinosaur trackway site at Red Fleet State Park to view *Grallator* and *Eubrontes* tracks.

Dinosaur track in the Triassic–Jurassic Nugget Sandstone along the shores of Red Fleet Reservoir. The Nugget Sandstone is mostly fossilized sand dunes exemplified by large-scale cross-beds; however, small interdune lake (oasis) and stream (wadi) deposits are also present in the Nugget Sandstone. The tracks at Red Fleet are near the top of the Nugget in stream deposits, possibly suggesting that dinosaurs found walking along streams easier than trudging across sand dunes; however, it may be more a matter of preservation. Tracks are nearly impossible to preserve in shifting sand.
Doug Sprinkel

The end of the Middle Jurassic and beginning of the Late Jurassic marked a time when the sea returned and deposited the Stump Formation. The Stump was deposited in a near-shore to shallow-marine environment that teemed with life. Belemnites, oysters, and ammonites are commonly preserved in the sandstone beds. A brief hiatus within the Stump interrupted marine deposition for about 1 million years, and another occurred again at the end of Stump deposition.

The last Jurassic unconformity formed locally on a surface that separates the Stump from the overlying Morrison Formation. Although the time between deposition of the two formations was brief, the depositional environments on either side of the unconformity are contrasting. The Stump Formation was deposited in a marine environment and the Morrison Formation was dominated by river and lake (fluvial and lacustrine) environments. Land animals, including a variety of dinosaurs, populated the Morrison landscape. Some geologists and paleontologists refer to the Morrison as the "real" Jurassic Park.

Crinoids are among the oldest animals still in existence. Dating back to the Middle Cambrian, approximately 510 million years ago, they are well documented in the fossil record. Although superficially plant-like in appearance, they are related to the sea stars.
Linda West

The huge, long-necked plant-eaters called "sauropods" were the most abundant dinosaurs of the Morrison environment. *Camarasaurus* was typical.
Linda West

ERA	SYSTEM	SERIES	FORMATIONS*		Thickness (feet) (not to scale)	LITHOLOGY	NOTES
Mesozoic			65 m.y.				
	Cretaceous	Upper	Mesaverde Group		2135-2625		Uplift of Uinta Mountains begins near end of Cretaceous and end of the Western Interior Seaway
			Baxter Shale	Mancos Shale	5905-6890		crinoid species *Uintacrinus* — large concretions — Fossil fish scales, ray finned fish, ammonites (cephalopods), and oysters (pelecypods)
			Frontier Sandstone		165-280		Dinosaurs (*Utahraptor, Gastonia, Deinonychus, Iguanodon,* and *Acrocanthosaurus*), cycadeoid trees, and pollen from newly emergent flowering plants
		Lower	Mowry Shale		30-230		K-0 unconformity, about 25 m.y. missing rock record
			Dakota Sandstone		50-265		Dinosaurs (*Allosaurus,* troodontid, *Camarasaurus, Diplodocus, Barosaurus, Apatosaurus, Haplocanthosaurus, Stegosaurus, Dryosaurus, Camptosaurus,* and *Ceratosaurus*), beetle traces, crocodiles, turtles, lizards, mammals, clams (pelecypods), and plants (cycads, ginkgos, conifers, ferns, horsetails)
			Cedar Mountain Formation		0-195		
	Jurassic	Upper	Morrison Formation		800-950		
			Stump Formation		130-265		
		Middle	Entrada Sandstone		50-250		Belemnites, sea stars, crinoids, clams, oysters, ammonites
			Carmel Formation		280-460		J-3 unconformity, about 1 m.y. missing rock record
		Lower	Nugget Sandstone		500-900		Dinosaur and pterosaur trace fossils (dinosaur tracks such as *Carmelopodus*), sea stars, ammonites, clams (pelecypods), and snails (gastropods)
	Triassic	Upper	Chinle Formation		280-410		Jurassic dinosaur tracks
							Triassic vertebrate tracks
		Lower	Moenkopi Formation		555-855		Dinosaur tracks, petrified wood, and the remains of a phytosaur (crocodile-like reptile); Gartra Member is at base
			Dinwoody Formation		0-540		Tr-3 unconformity, about 15 m.y. missing rock record
	251 m.y.						Tr-1 unconformity, about 21 m.y. missing rock record

(200 m.y. marker at left; 145 m.y. marker at left)

*Where side-by-side, formations on the left are restricted to the north flank of the Uinta Mountains and formations on the right are restricted to the south flank.

Doug Sprinkel

Cigars of the Sea?

Belemnites are often called "cigar fossils" due to their shape. However, like ammonites, they were cephalopods, related to the modern-day squid and octopus. This specimen of *Pachyteuthis densis* was collected from the Jurassic Stump Formation.

Pachyteuthis densis from the Stump Formation. In life, this and other belemnites probably resembled modern squid.
Left: FHPR specimen 1089/Courtesy UFH
Below: Linda West

Ancient Sea Monsters

Marine reptiles such as the ichthyosaurs and the long-necked plesiosaurs are found in the Jurassic Stump Formation. They are often mistaken for dinosaurs, but although these groups co-existed throughout the Mesozoic Era, there is only a distant connection.

Linda West

160 Million Years of Success

Dinosaurs first arose in the Late Triassic Period, about 225 million years ago. They quickly became the dominant land animals, successfully taking over niches previously filled by a group of "mammal-like" reptiles known as the therapsids. One important reason for the dinosaurs' success was the way in which the legs were positioned directly under the body. This unique style would help dinosaurs gain speed, agility, and weight-bearing advantages, as well as the ability to travel long distances.

Cast of *Stegosaurus stenops* in the Utah Field House of Natural History.
Linda West

After a period of no sediment deposition for 25 million years, stream and lake conditions returned about 120 million years ago in Early Cretaceous time with deposition of the Cedar Mountain Formation. The Cedar Mountain is a fluvial and lacustrine unit that contains dinosaur remains and the fossil pollen of the first flowering plants (angiosperms).

Utahraptor belonged to a family of dinosaurs known as the "dromaeosaurs," characterized by large retractable claws on the hind feet used for killing prey. Its discovery coincided with the release of the movie *Jurassic Park*, which portrayed a "raptor" about the actual size of this dinosaur.

Linda West

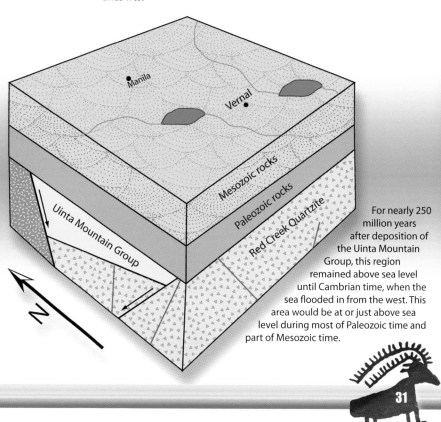

For nearly 250 million years after deposition of the Uinta Mountain Group, this region remained above sea level until Cambrian time, when the sea flooded in from the west. This area would be at or just above sea level during most of Paleozoic time and part of Mesozoic time.

Above: Multi-hued mudstones and shales characterize the Morrison Formation, which some people liken to "melting neapolitan ice cream."
Linda West

Below: Cedar Mountain Formation through Frontier Sandstone above Steinaker Reservoir.
Ron Stewart

Depositional patterns began to change during Dakota Sandstone time. The Dakota records the transition from fluvial deposition to coastal marsh as the great Cretaceous Western Interior Seaway began to flood the region about 100 million years ago. By the time the Mowry Shale was deposited, the region was fully submerged by the Cretaceous sea and abundant schools of fish swam in its waters. A profusion of fish scales is preserved in the Mowry, which attests to the fish population at that time. For about 25 million years (Mowry to Mesaverde Formations), the Cretaceous seaway dominated the landscape. By the end of Mesaverde deposition, however, the landscape had changed again. This region that had hovered around sea level since Mississippian time—being submerged for most of the Paleozoic, part of the Jurassic, and most of the Cretaceous—started to rise. The seabed warped upward in latest Cretaceous time, causing the sea to retreat and the seabed to reach the surface. The uplift would be so complete that the sea would never inundate the region again. The mountain-building event of the Laramide orogeny had begun!

THE RISE OF THE UINTA MOUNTAINS

The Laramide orogeny created the structural features that deformed the bedrock and set the stage for the spectacular landscape seen all along the Byway. Its intermittent, yet persistent, compressional deformation (squeezing) for about 35 million years folded and faulted the rocks. The dominant Laramide structures in the region are the Uinta arch and related Uinta fault zone. The Uinta arch is a great asymmetrical fold that has a length along its crest of about 160 miles, an average width of thirty miles, and generally coincides with the Uinta Mountains. The rocks on the north flank dip more steeply than the rocks on the south flank, giving the fold its asymmetry. The Uinta arch consists of two domes that are aligned east to west and separated by a shallow structural swale. The swale is crossed by U.S. Highway 191–Utah State Road 44 between Vernal and Manila, Utah. The Uinta arch is bounded on the north by a series of steeply dipping fault segments of the North Flank, Uinta, and Sparks fault zones, and on the south by the South Flank and Willow Creek fault zones.

The Scenic Byway crosses the Uinta fault zone segment on the north flank of the Uinta arch. Consequently, all of the rocks dip (or tilt) generally northward and increase in north dip as they approach the Uinta fault zone. A great thickness of Neoproterozoic Uinta Mountain Group was uplifted from the south along the fault and pushed against Mississippian and Pennsylvanian rocks. This structure can be seen in the Sheep Creek Canyon Geological Area, near the western boundary of Flaming Gorge National Recreation Area, along Utah State Road 44.

Above: Sheep Creek Canyon provides some of the most dramatic views of the Uinta Fault zone. Nearly vertical beds of Mississippian Madison Limestone form the high ridge at center, with later Paleozoic strata to the right and the Neoproterozoic Uinta Mountain Group on the left. Looking north from viewpoint about 0.6 miles beyond Palisades Memorial Park.
Linda West

Below: Near the end of the Cretaceous Period, compressional forces intermittently, yet persistently, uplifted the Uinta Mountains along a series of faults. The uplift warped the rocks to form a large asymmetrical fold called the Uinta arch. Adjacent to the rising Uinta Mountains were two basins. Each basin contained a freshwater lake that in time became saline. The Green River Formation is made of the lithified deposits of these lakes.

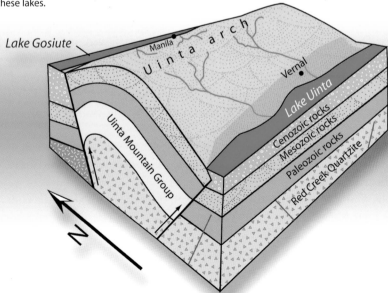

A Squid With a Twist

Ammonites belong to a group known as the cephalopods, literally meaning the "head-foot." Although ammonites went extinct at the end of the Cretaceous Period, their relatives the squid, octopus, and nautilus are still an important part of today's marine environments. Ammonites are used worldwide as index fossils. Index fossils are species that have a wide geographic distribution but a relatively short geologic existence, making them good indicators of the relative age of a unit.

Prionocyclus wyomingensis from the Frontier Formation.
FHPR specimen 725/Courtesy UFH

ERA	SYSTEM	SERIES	FORMATIONS*	Thickness (feet) (not to scale)	LITHOLOGY	NOTES
Cenozoic	Quaternary	Holocene	Unconsolidated deposits	less than 150		Alpine glaciers in Uinta Mountains and Green River connects to Colorado River system
		Pleistocene	South Flank piedmont alluvium	less than 30		
		Pliocene — 5 m.y.	Browns Park Formation	0-1640		Crustal relaxation; Uinta Mountains down-dropped along Uinta fault zone and drainage patterns change in eastern Uintas; capture of Green River and diversion into Red Canyon-Browns Park
	— 1.8 m.y.	Miocene				
		— 23 m.y.	Bishop Conglomerate	0-300		
		Oligocene	Starr Flat Member of Duchesne River Formation	130-755		
			Lapoint Member of Duchesne River Formation	390		Uinta Mountains uplift ends and crustal stability begins; Gilbert Peak erosion surface forms and Bishop Conglomerate is deposited; Uinta Mountain Group is well exposed
	Tertiary	34 m.y.	Dry Gulch Creek Member of Duchesne River Formation	less than 500		
			Brennan Basin Member of Duchesne River Formation	720-1970		
		Eocene	Bridger Formation / Uinta Formation	200-2445		Contains gilsonite deposits in Uinta Basin
						Mahogany oil shale zone
			Green River Formation	1380-3840		Uinta Mountains continue to uplift and erode; creation of Lakes Gosiute (Green River Basin) and Uinta (Unita Basin) as the basins continue to subside
			Wasatch Formation	985-3020		Uinta Mountains continue to uplift and erode, locally exposing the Uinta Mountain Group; subsidence of Green River and Uinta Basins
		— 56 m.y.				
		Paleocene	Fort Union Formation / Flagstaff Member of Green River Formation	230-2950		
	65 m.y.					Unconformity, about 6 m.y. missing rock record; TK boundary and the extinction of dinosaurs

*Formations in gray are not exposed along the Scenic Byway but are exposed in the area.
*Where side-by-side, formations on the left are restricted to the north flank of the Uinta Mountains and formations on the right are restricted to the south flank.

Doug Sprinkel

Following the fault zone eastward, the Uinta Mountain Group is pushed against Pennsylvanian–Permian Weber Sandstone along the Flaming Gorge Reservoir south of Beehive Point and against Triassic–Jurassic Nugget Sandstone, along U.S. Highway 191, a few miles north of the dam.

Subsidiary, steeply dipping faults are exposed north of the Uinta fault zone, including an unnamed set of faults along lower Sheep Creek Canyon and the Henrys Fork fault zone north of and around Manila. The faults in the lower Sheep Creek Canyon area cut Triassic and Jurassic rocks. The Henrys Fork fault zone consists of two branches. The south branch placed Cretaceous Baxter Shale against Tertiary Wasatch Formation near Manila. The north branch of the Henrys Fork fault is exposed on the peninsula from Linwood Bay north to the Lucerne Valley Marina. There, it placed the Upper Cretaceous Mesaverde Group over the Tertiary Wasatch Formation. Both sets of faults in lower Sheep Creek Canyon and near Manila have much less displacement than the Uinta fault and were likely formed near the end of the Laramide uplift.

BASINS AND LARGE LAKES

Two basins formed on either side of the rising highlands: the Green River Basin on the north, and the Uinta Basin on the south. Both basins caught the erosional debris shed off the Uinta Mountains. This debris lithified (hardened into rock), forming the uppermost part of the Late Cretaceous Mesaverde Group and the overlying units through the Eocene Wasatch Formation. Near the end of Wasatch Formation deposition, however, two brackish-to-saline lakes—Lake Gosiute on the north and Lake Uinta on the south—formed and flooded the Green River and Uinta Basins, respectively, depositing the Green River Formation.

Throughout the late Wasatch Formation and early Green River Formation history, a dance of dominance was played out between the two formations. Coarse-grained deposits typical of the Wasatch Formation were able to push the margins of Lake Gosiute northward and those of Lake Uinta southward during periods of uplift and possible climatic change. Periods of little uplift, and a possibly wetter climate, allowed the Green River Formation to flood the mountain front, covering the Wasatch beds. Ultimately the Green River Formation won—at least temporarily. A similar dance of dominance played out between the upper Green River Formation and overlying Eocene formations (the Bridger Formation in the Green River Basin and the Duchesne River Formation in the Uinta Basin). This time the Green River Formation lost and Lakes Gosiute and Uinta eventually dried up about 45 to 44 million years ago.

EARLY STREAM DEVELOPMENT IN THE EASTERN UINTA MOUNTAINS

Crustal stability replaced basin subsidence and the Uinta Mountains uplift about 30 million years ago. Consequently, an extensive, gently sloping surface (pediment) called the Gilbert Peak erosion surface developed around the flanks of the highland, leaving only the higher parts of the range above the surface. Streams flowed away from the highlands in a radial pattern and across the surrounding broad plain. At this time, the Green River likely did not cut through the Uintas as it does now. The Bishop Conglomerate was deposited on the Gilbert Peak erosion surface. The Bishop Conglomerate is well exposed on the south flank of the Uinta Mountains, but does not seem to be preserved on the north flank of the Uinta Mountains in the area crossed by the Scenic Byway.

This period of crustal stability and the radial drainage pattern did not last long. The Uinta Mountains began to feel the effects of regional extension (stretching). This episode of extension probably began about 25 million years ago in late Oligocene time, but most of the movement likely took place about 15 to 10 million years ago in Miocene time. During this time, normal faults and reactivated Laramide faults displaced Tertiary rocks and warped and faulted the Gilbert Peak erosion surface. Downward movement on the Uinta fault zone lowered the eastern Uinta Mountains and tilted the range north and east. The radial drainage system was also altered. Soon after the initial lowering and tilting of the eastern Uinta Mountains, a new east-trending drainage developed along the former crest of the Uinta Mountains, forming a juvenile Red Canyon and the valley of Browns Park. The new Red Canyon creek flowed east and divided the former north-flowing streams, causing the streams on the north side of the Red Canyon creek to reverse their flow southward. Initial deposition of the Browns Park Formation began on the deformed Gilbert Peak erosion surface and filled in the newly created river valley.

As mentioned earlier, the Green River likely did not cut through the Uinta Mountains as it does now prior to Miocene time; instead, it flowed out of the Wind River Mountains to Green River, Wyoming (as it does today), but then turned eastward through southern Wyoming. Some geologists speculate that this ancestral Green River flowed to the North Platte River and was part of the Mississippi River drainage system. However, by early Pleistocene time (perhaps 1 to 2 million years ago) the new Red Canyon creek drainage had incised its way north by headward erosion and captured the Green River. The Green River then flowed south to the Uinta Mountains through Red Canyon and into Browns Park, which continued to fill with deposits. Evidence suggests that Browns Park was a closed basin and the Green River was still not connected to the Colorado River system at this time.

GREEN RIVER AND COLORADO RIVER CONNECTION

We know that eventually the Green River connected to the Colorado River system through Lodore Canyon, but how and when is still up for debate. Two prevailing ideas are presented in the geologic literature (see Hansen, 1986). One idea suggests that the Green River continued to fill the closed Browns Park valley with sediment until the sediment fill reached a threshold that allowed water to spill over the valley rim on the south, diverting the Green River southward through the ancestral Lodore Canyon. This canyon was likely in the upper reaches of the Colorado River system that flowed to an area lower in elevation compared to Browns Park, and now served as a drain to remove large volumes of sediment from Browns Park. In addition, the increased water flow enlarged and deepened the canyon to carve Lodore Canyon to its present depth.

The other idea suggests that headward erosion by streams of the Colorado River system from the south methodically captured and incorporated local streams, perhaps aided by renewed faulting that slightly changed drainage divides. Eventually, a small yet vigorous stream in the ancestral Lodore Canyon cut its way into Browns Park, capturing the Green River. Similar to the previously discussed idea, the increased water flow eventually enlarged and deepened the small canyon, carving the Lodore Canyon we see today. Either way, the Green River became part of the Colorado River system with a lower base-level elevation that caused entrenchment along its course. In all likelihood, the Green River connected with the Colorado River system in early Pleistocene time, perhaps less than a million years ago.

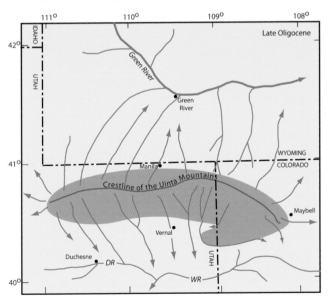

Late Oligocene time. A radial drainage pattern formed, which drained the highlands of the Uinta Mountains into the adjoining basins. Note that the Green River did not flow south to the Uinta Mountains, but east into south-central Wyoming.

Doug Sprinkel

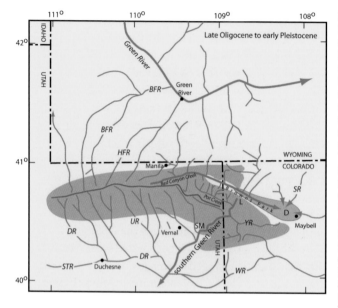

Late Oligocene to early Pleistocene time. The radial drainage was altered as the eastern Uinta Mountains subsided and tilted northeasterly, and a new drainage formed along the former crestline. The new Red Canyon creek bifurcated north-flowing streams and redirected their flow southeastward to the newly formed closed basin (D) of Browns Park. The Snake River (SR) also flowed to Browns Park. The Green River still flowed eastward, but headward erosion by a tributary of the Red Canyon creek began to cut its way north. The Blacks Fork River (BFR) and Henrys Fork River (HFR) flowed north to the Green River. Headward erosion by the southern Green River had cut Split Mountain (SM), and likely, into Lodore Canyon (L). Headward erosion was inching the Yampa River (YR) toward Browns Park. The Duchesne River (DR), Uinta River (UR), Strawberry River (STR), and White River (WR) were well established.

Doug Sprinkel

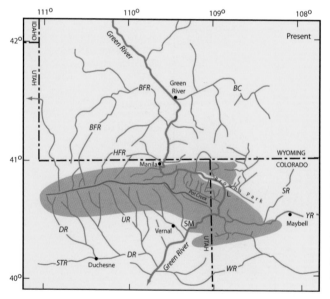

Present time. Capture of the Green River at Green River, Wyoming, in early Pleistocene time, sent its waters south to the Uinta Mountains and into Browns Park. This also altered the flow of the Blacks Fork (BFR) and Henrys Fork (HFR) rivers. The abandoned part of the Green River east of Green River, Wyoming, reversed flow and became Bitter Creek (BC). Less than a million years ago, water flowed across the divide and into Lodore Canyon (L), connecting the Green River to the Colorado River system. In addition, the Yampa River (YR) cut its way into Browns Park near Maybell, Colorado. All diagrams are modified from Hansen (1986).

Doug Sprinkel

THE FINAL GEOLOGIC CHAPTER?

Part of the last chapter in the geologic story of this region includes periods of Pleistocene glaciation (about 660,000 to 12,000 years ago) of the higher parts of the Uinta Mountains, continued headward erosion, and entrenchment of streams. The region is still under the influence of tectonic extension. Although this area has not recently experienced an earthquake, some evidence on the Diamond Mountain Plateau suggests that earthquakes large enough to break the ground surface have occurred within the past 150,000 years. It is possible that this region could experience another moderate earthquake in the future. No one knows for sure how the landscape will change, but it is certain that it will change, and along with it, the plant and animal communities that live on what we call geology.

DESERT TO TREELINE

Plant Communities of the Byway
Tom Elder

Geology Shapes Biology

The effect of geology on soil type and plants is readily seen on the ridges near Steinaker Reservoir. A pattern of Utah juniper and other woody shrubs typifies the Mowry Shale and Dakota Sandstone. It appears that the highly fractured shales of the Mowry store water, while below, the sandy soils developed on the Dakota provide good soil conditions. In contrast, the Frontier siltstones, along with the Cedar Mountain and Morrison Formation shales, are comparatively barren of plant life. In this way, geology controls biology. Each formation sets the stage for a unique biotic community by creating conditions that insure the success of certain plant species, and the failure of others.

A short way north, on Red Mountain, the coarse Gartra Member of the Chinle Formation produces permeable, fractured ledges that make a good ponderosa pine habitat if there is sufficient soil moisture. The red shaley Moenkopi below produces a dense clay soil that is largely impermeable to water, effectively trapping moisture in the Gartra. This combination sustains a magnificent ponderosa forest perched on the Gartra ledge, above a very different juniper woodland on the Moenkopi. The only other rock layer that supports extensive ponderosa forests along the Byway is the Uinta Mountain Group, which offers similar sandstone-over-shale conditions.

(See pages 40–41) The slopes above Steinaker Reservoir show how different strata affect plant growth. Almost nothing grows on the clay of the Cedar Mountain Formation (bottom), but the Dakota Sandstone just above it supports a band of Utah juniper and a few ponderosa pines.
Ron Stewart/Courtesy UDWR

As you drive from Vernal or Manila up to the Byway's summit at the Uintah County and Daggett County line, the scenery changes in two distinct ways. The first change is geological, as you drive "back in time," into older and older formations as described in the geology chapter. The second change is ecological, as you rise through a predictable succession of different plant and animal life. Long ago, a scientist named Merriam called these "life zones," and correctly noted that they reflect the increasing amounts of water and decreasing temperatures at higher altitude. This chapter will focus on "plant communities," each one dominated by a few species that set the stage for the other life forms that can exist there.

Eight plant communities are commonly recognized along the Byway. From the lowest elevation to the highest, they are: desert shrub, pinyon-juniper, mountain shrub, ponderosa, aspen-lodgepole, Douglas-fir, subalpine, and alpine. Of course, the different plant communities are not separated by sharp, vivid boundaries. Each one's elevation range overlaps with those above and below, and the edges are usually blurry, with plants from different communities mingling. This "edge effect" produces the greatest diversity of species, and makes the edges good places to look for wildlife as well as changes in the plants.

DESERT SHRUB COMMUNITY

The desert shrub community only forms at the lowest elevations near Vernal and Manila, usually below 6,500 feet. It is subjected to harsh summer heat, yet is often quite cold and snowy in winter. Though the temperature varies widely, precipitation is predictably low, averaging less than ten inches per year. Adaptations for this demanding habitat include small leaf surfaces to reduce water loss (e.g., saltbush), long roots to reach a deep water table (sagebrush), fleshy leaves or stems to store

The edible bulbs of the sego lily (*Calochortus nuttallii*), Utah's state flower, were a staple of Native American diets and also helped early pioneers survive until their crops were in. To cope with ground-cracking dryness, sego lilies have very narrow leaves that help reduce water loss.
Nancy Bostick-Ebbert

Frigid winters limit the number of cactus species that can grow here, but claret cup cactus (*Echinocereus sp.*) brightens sandstone outcrops with showy wine-red blossoms.
Nancy Bostick-Ebbert

The drought-adapted joint fir or Mormon tea (*Ephedra sp.*) is nearly leafless, relying mainly on its green stems for photosynthesis. Both Native Americans and the pioneers brewed a medicinal tea from it.
Nancy Bostick-Ebbert

water (cactus), and fast life cycles during wetter springs, leaving resistant seeds to endure the summer heat and drought (annual wildflowers).

Big sagebrush, greasewood, and saltbush are dominant plants, with soil salinity strongly affecting the proportions of each species. Greasewood (*Sarcobatus vermiculatus*) dominates the lowest, saltiest environments; sagebrush (*Artemisia* species) requires soils that are not very saline; and saltbush (*Atriplex* species) falls somewhere in between. North of Steinaker Reservoir, for example, bright green greasewood dominates the middle of Steinaker Draw, while the blue-gray of sagebrush cloaks the higher, "fresher" soils at the edges of the draw. Greasewood leaves resemble short, fleshy needles, and their salty tissue is not eaten by many animals. Sagebrush, as a palatable evergreen (it does not lose its leaves seasonally), is heavily browsed by mule deer in the winter, when there is precious little else to eat.

Unfortunately, older sagebrushes are declining over large parts of the West, and young ones are not replacing them. This crisis is likely caused by a combination of overgrazing, exotic species, climate change, and probably other unknown factors.

Indian ricegrass (*Oryzopsis sp.*) is a good example of native bunchgrasses, which grow in scattered clumps rather than as continuous ground covers. Mule deer graze on ricegrass, and its seeds are important to many small mammals and birds.
Ron Stewart/Courtesy UDWR

Spring Cheater

The name "cheatgrass" pretty much sums up Westerners' feelings about *Bromus tectorum*, an exotic species accidentally introduced from Eurasia. As a winter annual, cheatgrass starts growth in the fall, maintains green tissue under winter snows, and is raring to go in the spring, getting a head start on the native plants. It steals nutrients and water from the natives as it runs through its growth in double-time. Then, it sets its seeds and dies, becoming useless as forage. Cheatgrass seeds are those annoying little hitchhikers that prick you through your socks and use you to move to new areas, and they can even injure the mouths of livestock and wildlife.

Ominously, these carpets of dried-up cheatgrass increase the fire frequency (the typical return interval of fire) of an ecosystem. For instance, the fire frequency for a specific sagebrush ecosystem north of Vernal might be about fifty years, meaning that, after a fire killed the sagebrush, there would be an average of five decades for sagebrush seeds to disperse and new plants to grow to full size. The roots of the native bunchgrasses, such as Indian ricegrass, normally survive fire, and temporarily dominate an area in the first years after a fire. This change—bunchgrass to sagebrush to fire and back to bunchgrass—was the normal pattern and maintained a healthy mix of bunchgrass and sagebrush.

However, the tinder-dry cheatgrass greatly reduces the time between fires, sometimes to as little as three to five years. After fueling a fire, the plant returns in force the very next year, and immediately sets the stage for a new fire. There is no time for sagebrush to return and grow to maturity. Slowly, whole Western landscapes change from productive sagebrush shrublands to barren cheatgrass deserts.

In ecology, there are no "good" or "bad" plants, just plants out of place, which we call weeds. Even cheatgrass pulls its weight in Eurasia. In Utah, cheatgrass seems likely to prosper in the coming age of a globally warming Earth. Our native sagebrush, bunchgrasses, wildlife, and ranchers may not fare as well.

Living Dirt

Under the desert shrub and pinyon-juniper communities, you will often find a frothy black frosting, like thousands of miniature towers and ridges, coating the ground. Called cryptobiotic ("hidden life") crust or simply soil crust, it is a whole community of microscopic life including nematodes, fungi, protozoans, photosynthetic bacteria, and many others. This invisible zoo comes fully to life when it rains, and goes dormant again when the crust dries.

Soil crusts can absorb the impact of a raindrop without buckling, and so protect the underlying sediments from washing away. This, in turn, also protects the root systems of the larger plants (such as sagebrush) that rise out of the soil crust. The crust cannot, however, withstand a 150-pound human treading a footprint into it. The resulting broken crust allows the sediments below to blow or wash away. That is why true desert rats (the human kind) walk in washes, stay on exposed bedrock, or stick to existing trails where possible. It is also why scarring by vehicles, or by too much traffic of any kind, is such a serious problem. Such scars accelerate erosion and take a long time to heal, even after the traffic stops.

Though these desert soils will never be farmed to produce a crop for human consumption, they do produce a crop for the wild animals. If we value the animals, both the ones we hunt and the ones we do not, we need to start with protection of the living dirt.

By holding together pockets of soil, cryptobiotic crusts help these junipers and other plants maintain a foothold on the slickrock around Red Fleet Reservoir.
Linda West

PINYON-JUNIPER COMMUNITY

Above the desert shrub community, at elevations of 5,500 to 7,500 feet, is a band dominated by junipers with varying proportions of pinyon pine. At lower elevations, this woodland is almost 100 percent Utah juniper (*Juniperus osteosperma*), while higher up, pinyon pine (*Pinus edulis*) becomes increasingly abundant. Pinyon pines are susceptible to frost damage, which limits both how high into the cooler mountains they can grow, and also how low, because in winter the sinking of frigid air into the valleys creates cold air inversions.

Scientists are finding that these "P-J" woodlands are surprisingly rich in bird species, with a high percentage of obligate species: those which depend on that vegetation type and cannot easily live in other types. One such obligate species is the pinyon jay, sometimes seen as roving, noisy flocks of "blue crows." These birds collect the pine nuts and stash them in the ground to be eaten later. In response, the pines produce unpredictable nut crops, forcing the jays to search out each year's bounty. A few nuts are not retrieved and sprout into new trees.

The junipers produce blueish berries that are eaten by coyotes and other animals, dispersing their seeds in the little fertilizer pile of their droppings. P-J woodlands also provide cover for mule deer and elk, which emerge from the pygmy forest to graze on the nearby sage grasslands.

(Right) The rigors of a harsh environment often shape Utah junipers into "natural bonsai." Ron Stewart
(Below) Over a long time, pinyon-juniper woods may form such a dense canopy that no understory plants can survive, and no "seedbank" of dormant grass and forb seeds remains in the soil. If fire then kills the trees, land managers may need to reseed the area, as was the case after the 2002 Mustang Ridge Fire north of Dutch John. Linda West

This view looking up the valley of Sheep Creek shows the influence of different soils and water supply on plant communities. In the foreground, junipers grow well on a phosphate-rich bed in the Park City Formation. Beyond that, the gray-to-red shales of the Dinwoody, Moenkopi, and Chinle Formations are largely barren, except where covered by sandy talus (fallen rubble) from the Nugget Sandstone cliffs at right. The entire area would normally be too dry for broad-leafed trees such as cottonwoods and willows, but along the creek they and a few large conifers form a narrow riparian (stream-dependent) woodland.
Linda West

Various species of paintbrush (*Castilleja sp.*) grow from desert to mountain elevations. All are semi-parasitic; their roots penetrate those of other plants such as sagebrush and steal nutrients from them.
Nancy Bostick-Ebbert

Sometimes called "easter daisy," *Townsendia* often dots dry, rocky soils at various elevations.
Nancy Bostick-Ebbert

Oldest Growth

When people think of old growth forest, they normally picture cathedral-like groves of tall, elegant trees such as redwoods. Paradoxically, the oldest of old growth along the Byway is probably those lowly Utah junipers eking out a scanty living on the rocky foothills. Locally, they are called "cedars," because they are rot-resistant like true cedars (genus *Cedrus*, not native to Utah). Many of them have had a massive limb cut off years ago by cowboys, to be used as a "cedar post" on a nearby barbed wire fence.

These "bonsai" Utah junipers—an acquired taste for many people—generally do best on the coarse, well-drained soils that crumble from sandstones, but they can grow in soils formed from almost any substrate, if given enough time.

The key to enough time is the absence of fire. Fires do not usually burn across sandstone bluffs or shale barrens, because such areas lack the light fuels (such as grasses) needed for the fire to spread. In such areas, junipers can take the hundreds of years they need to reach their full stature. In valley soils, they will establish, but sooner or later a range fire will kill them. Since humans have been suppressing fires for the last hundred years or so, "young" junipers have been creeping out into these formerly grassy areas. Unless fires or human woodcutting intervene, the invaders will eventually turn sage grasslands into juniper woodlands.

In the past, the Bureau of Land Management has "chained" pinyon-juniper forests to reverse these trends, and to benefit the understory plants. A heavy chain is strung between two bulldozers, and as they drive across the landscape, the chain knocks down all of the trees in the path. Such an area is visible at the Dinosaur Trackway trailhead, where junipers were chained in the 1970s, and later, the invading young junipers were "lopped and scattered" in 2005.

(Above) Growing from desert to middle mountain elevations, sagebrush provides important forage for mule deer, and is the main item in the diets of sage grouse and pronghorn.

Ron Stewart

(Below) The elegant spring flower clusters of chokecherry (*Prunus virginiana*) will later become dark cherry-like fruits, relished by many birds and mammals.

Linda West

Mountain Shrub Community

The mountain shrub community forms a band of open country at varied elevations between the pinyon-juniper and higher mountain forests. It is dominated by low (less than ten feet tall) shrubs that include mountain mahogany, serviceberry, chokecherry, snowberry, sagebrush, bitterbrush, and many others. Grasses and forbs (short, broad-leaved plants without woody stems, such as daisies and buttercups) grow beneath the bushes. Often steep and rocky, this vegetation zone can be difficult for a person to travel through, and long pants are essential to keep from being extensively scratched.

This is summer range for mule deer, and the current health of these plants has a lot to do with how large the year's deer herd is. Many of these shrubs grow spiny twigs to discourage deer from stripping them completely, but many still offer essential resources for a variety of life.

Saskatoon serviceberry, for instance, provides nectar to pollinators in spring, frequently hosts tent caterpillars and fungus in summer, and produces a fall fruit that many animals consume. Though often overlooked by humans, the mountain shrub community is vastly important to the wildlife of the Byway.

The leaves, twigs, and fruit of serviceberry (*Amelanchier alnifolia*) provide food for many kinds of wildlife, from moose to mountain chickadees.
Linda West

PONDEROSA COMMUNITY

Ponderosa pines (*Pinus ponderosa*) may be the most majestic trees on the Byway, commonly attaining diameters of up to three feet and heights of up to eighty, occasionally even one hundred, feet. Adult ponderosas are widely spaced, with a rich and diverse understory of many of the same plants seen in the mountain shrub community, including the all-important sagebrush.

Ponderosa is well adapted to cope with fire, with adult trees shielded by thick, corky bark that will char but not burn easily. In addition, the lower branches prune themselves as the tree grows, with the higher remaining branches beyond the reach of ground fires. When a fire burns the accumulated fuels on the ground below, the photosynthetic crown of the ponderosa remains unscathed. In fact, the reduced competition for soil and water invigorates the adult trees, though young ones may be killed.

If enough time passes, junipers and pinyon pines move into the newly burned area, forming "ladder fuels" that allow fire to climb upward into the branches of adult ponderosas, killing them. Thus, relatively frequent ground fires help maintain these attractive, open woodlands. Many years of fire suppression can, paradoxically, result in destructive crown fires.

The U.S. Forest Service has been aggressively acting to restore the "fire balance" in the extensive ponderosa forests of the Flaming Gorge area. Actions include removing beetle-killed trees, thinning young pines, and setting frequent "prescribed fires" to reduce the amount of fuel on the forest floor. Some lightning-caused fires are also allowed to burn if they meet certain requirements. Historic fire frequency is being calculated by measuring the number of "fire scars" in the tree-ring record of felled trees. It appears that the fire frequency in the Flaming Gorge ponderosa forests is about twenty to thirty years. In hotter and drier ponderosa forests, such as in Arizona, it can be as high as every seven years.

Though most ponderosa woodlands occur at elevations of 7,000 to 8,000 feet, soil conditions are very important to where these pines will actually grow. Ponderosa pine tends to prosper on acidic, sandy, or rocky soils produced by sandstones, such as on the broad Uinta Mountain Group benchland of the Greendale area.

From spring to early summer, arrowleaf balsamroot (*Balsamorhiza sagittata*) can turn dry uplands gold with its sunflower-like blooms. Deer, elk, and bighorn sheep all graze on it.
Linda West

(Opposite) By killing off young trees but leaving the adult pines unharmed, small ground fires help maintain the open, park-like appearance of ponderosa woods, such as these along the Red Canyon rim.
Linda West

ASPEN-LODGEPOLE COMMUNITY

The quaking aspen (*Populus tremuloides*) is Utah's most common deciduous tree (one that loses its leaves in the winter). Easily recognized by its creamy-white bark, aspen is actually a species of mountain cottonwood, and though it occurs at elevations of 7,500 to 10,000 feet, it is close kin to the Fremont cottonwoods that grow far below along the Green River.

Aspen forms groves, more properly called "clones," each started from a single seed that sprouted ages ago. Once established, the tree develops a mass of roots that send up new trunks. Each trunk in the clone is genetically identical to all of the other trunks, and, as they are all connected by the roots, what looks like multiple trees is actually a single large organism. Fire, avalanche, or logging kills the tree trunks—but not the hidden roots. Twigs in the tree's crown produce auxin, a hormone that suppresses the roots from sending up new saplings ("suckers"). If the crown is killed, auxin is no longer sent to the roots, which then produce a thicket of suckers that can grow as much as four feet per year. Individual trunks have a relatively short life span (about eighty to one hundred years), but through its roots and suckers, aspen attains a kind of plant immortality. Some scientists speculate that our current clones may be thousands of years old, having been established at the end of the last glacial retreat about 10,000 years ago.

An aspen grove is often a single organism called a clone, with multiple trunks all springing from one root system. Larger stands of aspens may include several clones, whose leaves "turn" at different times in autumn, revealing where one clone ends and another begins. Ron Stewart

The Death of Aspen

Aspens are declining rapidly in many western states, and the U.S. Forest Service is not sure what to do about it. In Utah, scientists predict that perhaps 10 percent of the aspens could die by 2010. As it is, aspens cover barely more than a tenth of Ashley National Forest, yet a disproportionate number of animals depend on them for a habitat.

The list of suspects in the death of aspen is a long one, and includes the following:

A century's worth of fire suppression in aspen clones, favoring shade-tolerant species.

Recurring droughts, which no doubt weaken aspen clones and make them more vulnerable to insects and disease.

Warmer winters that seem to make it easier for aspen-attacking insects and fungus to move to higher altitudes and remain active for a longer part of the year. It may be more difficult for aspen to move upwards, due to how infrequently its seeds germinate.

Overgrazing of aspen suckers by livestock or wildlife.

Most likely, a combination of all these culprits is at work.

Aspens are often called "quakies" (their species name, *tremuloides*, comes from the Latin word meaning "trembling") because their leaves quiver at the slightest breeze. They are a wonderful sight in the fall as the leaves change from green to yellow, and finally gold. Since different clones start "turning" at different times, this is when you can see where one clone ends and another begins.

Many birds nest in aspen branches and trunks, and herbivores such as beaver, elk, and porcupine eat the twigs and bark, especially of the saplings. Aspens let abundant sunlight reach the forest floor, allowing many wildflowers to grow; deer and elk also find good grazing in the sunny clones.

Aspen wood is light and soft, not strong or durable enough to be useful as lumber, but some mills process it for particle board, toothpicks, small boxes, or paper pulp.

Although it has thin bark and even a light fire can kill the adult trees, aspen is a fire-adapted plant, because the next year, a thicket of suckers will spring up.

Lodgepole pine (*Pinus contorta*), the other dominant tree of this community, copes with fire equally well but in a different way.

Named for its straight, thin trunks that made ideal supports for Native American tipis, lodgepole pine often forms dense "dog-hair" thickets. These contain crowded, relatively small trees (thirty to fifty feet tall), which so completely exclude light as to have no understory. Such thickets often start with a "stand-replacing fire," a crown fire that kills all of the existing trees. As one of the best examples of a fire-adapted species, lodgepole is prepared for such an event with "serotinous" cones.

These cones are gummed shut with resin, but the heat of a fire causes them to open and release their seeds. Falling unharmed to the blackened ground, the seeds have abundant sunshine and little or no competition with other plants for water and nutrients. In other words, fire creates ideal circumstances for lodgepole growth. In such a stand-replacing event, a vast army of new seedlings, all the same age (a population known as a "cohort"), springs up to renew the forest. After the Yellowstone National Park fires of 1988, biologists routinely documented 1,000 new lodgepole seedlings per acre.

Lodgepole pines form typical "dog-hair" stands near the summit of the Byway. The young lodgepoles in front have grown up after a small fire was followed by logging.
Linda West

In the absence of such a fire, the identically-aged cohort matures together, and eventually starts falling victim to the afflictions of old age. The weakened older trees are often hit by infestations of mountain pine beetles, which lay their eggs in the living inner bark (cambium). The larvae tunnel through the cambium layer, girdling and often killing the tree, then emerge as adult beetles to mate and lay eggs for another cycle in other trees. Epidemics of mountain pine beetle appear to be a normal feature in the Uintas, occurring every century or so. As the trees die and topple over, the heavy fuel they provide on the forest floor virtually guarantees an eventual stand-replacing fire, and so the cycle is repeated.

Lodgepole trunks are usually too thin to be milled into boards, but in some areas the trees are harvested for use in log construction. Like fire, logging can stimulate reseeding, because the cones are crushed and scattered in the debris (slash) left behind, and seedlings quickly germinate. But in fairness, unmanaged lodgepole thickets do have ecological value. For example, they provide thermal cover for animals, being far warmer under the closed canopy in the winter, and far cooler in the summer.

Though more at home in the moister mountains of the Northwest, Douglas-fir finds a few places, especially on limestone outcrops, that can meet its needs here.
Ron Stewart/ Courtesy UDWR

Douglas-fir Community

Douglas-fir (*Pseudotsuga menziesii*) is one of America's important timber trees, but grows largest in areas wetter and milder than the Uintas, such as the Cascades of Washington and Oregon. Along the Byway, it grows best in comparatively moist, yet also comparatively warm and sunny, locations, at elevations of 7,500 to 8,500 feet.

Douglas-fir also has a decided preference for basic (as opposed to acidic) soil conditions, which are normally present on soils derived from limestones. For

Cold temperatures and strong winds determine the treeline, where the subalpine forest comes to a distinct end on the higher mountain slopes.
Ron Stewart/Courtesy UDWR

example, Douglas-firs dominate the Madison Limestone outcrops around the Bassett Springs trailheads, but farther north, on the sandstone and shale of the Lodore Formation, the subalpine community of Engelmann spruce and subalpine fir prevails.

Since the latter two species are shade-tolerant, they can grow under mature Douglas-firs, and will in time replace them (a process called succession). Occasional fires prevent the subalpine trees from totally eliminating Douglas-firs. On the other hand, if stands are clearcut and create very sunny conditions, aspens and lodgepole pines may move in. Selective logging of only the largest Douglas-firs may help to maintain this community.

SUBALPINE COMMUNITY

This community's trees, Engelmann spruce (*Picea engelmannii*) and subalpine fir (*Abies lasiocarpa*), require moist, cool, and shady conditions. They intermingle with lodgepoles and Douglas-firs by growing in the shade of those trees, but are found extensively at elevations from 10,000 to 11,000 feet. The spruce-fir forest is dark and cool, and a pleasure to walk into.

After they mature, the only trees that can germinate in their shade are their own offspring, so in many of the higher areas of the Uintas, spruce-fir is the climax community—one that will maintain itself until some disturbance (such as logging or fire) removes the adults. Given the climate and short summers, the fire frequency in such areas is very low, measured in centuries rather than decades. If disturbed, the forest is very slow in returning, especially at sites close to the timberline.

These trees must endure heavy snowfalls without limbs breaking, so they have a narrow pyramidal shape like a Swiss chalet to shed snow. This also increases the effective precipitation by accumulating snow piles beneath, and shading them from the sun. In spring and summer, these patchy snowbanks alternate with wet duff from rotting logs, and a sparse ground cover of low berry bushes such as grouse whortleberry (*Vaccinium scoparium*). In favorable situations, the subalpine forest may be more than one hundred feet tall, and is true old-growth forest, with many standing snags and downed trunks. At the forest's uppermost elevation limit is the treeline, where trees abruptly give way to the short, ground-hugging plants of the alpine community.

Utah's state tree, the blue spruce, grows along streams at lower elevations. It can be distinguished from Engelmann spruce by its habitat, more symmetrical crown shape, and much larger cones.

ALPINE COMMUNITY

The alpine community (commonly called tundra) is found above the treeline, from about 11,000 feet on up. This is a rigorous environment; it is cold, windy, and surprisingly dry. In addition to breaking the branches and snow-blasting the leaves, wind tends to dry plants out, sucking moisture from the leaves. In winter, there is often a lot of snow, but in summer it can become quite dry and sun-baked. Also, the average annual temperature is so low that a short distance below the surface, the ground remains frozen (permafrost) essentially year-round, preventing deep root growth. Since recovering from damage under these conditions is an agonizingly slow process, it is important that human visitors stay on trails as much as possible.

The result of these stresses is a Lilliputian world—tiny grasses, forbs, lichens, mosses, and wildflowers—that you must get down on your hands and knees to fully appreciate. Most alpine plants are perennials, and many of them grow as low, stemless "cushion plants," such as moss campion, thus avoiding the strong winds blowing a few inches above. Also look for splashes of what looks like paint on the rocks. These are lichens, symbiotic associations of an alga species to photosynthesize, and a fungus species to absorb water and minerals. Lichens very slowly break rock down into sediment, and are present in all the plant communities, but perhaps most visible in the alpine tundra.

The wildflower bloom lasts from June through August, and later autumn visitors find instead a dry, brown landscape of plants retreating into dormancy. Although the Byway itself does not pass through the alpine community, you can walk into it from the trailhead above Hacking Lake, which is a fairly rough thirty-minute drive west of the Byway along the Red Cloud Loop road.

Above the treeline, lichens, mosses, and tiny flowering plants cling to rocks and hug the ground.
Ron Stewart/Courtesy UDWR

Ron Stewart

GRAB THE BINOCULARS

Wildlife of the Byway

Mary Beth Bennis-Smith and Ron Stewart

Those who spend time in wild places know that the presence of wildlife provides charm to any outdoor experience. Experiences range from the most humble in nature, like simply listening to bird song, to the extraordinary event of watching the playful antics of bighorn lambs. In whatever way wild animals share their presence, their company makes our time outdoors all the richer.

The Byway is home to many wild creatures, and you are encouraged to discover them as part of your experience. Remember, most wild animals are not comfortable making their presence known to humans, but following the simple techniques described below and stopping at the recommended locations will increase your chances of observing wildlife.

WILDLIFE VIEWING TIPS

1. As a general rule, wildlife will be more numerous and active at both dawn and dusk. Although many animals are chiefly either nocturnal (active at night) or diurnal (active in the day), the transitional times of dawn and dusk provide more viewing opportunities. **From dusk to dawn, please drive with special care and watch for animals crossing the road.**

Seasons also affect the movements and visibility of wildlife. Large game such as deer and elk are likely to be seen at lower elevations in winter than in summer. Many bird species are found here only in the summer breeding season, while some simply pass through during spring and fall migrations.

2. Whether you view wildlife from your vehicle or on foot will depend on your time, physical abilities, and the degree to which you wish to experience wildlife. A car

serves the dual purpose of being both a "blind," since many wild animals are acclimated to traffic, and an area for safe viewing. This viewing strategy is most useful when large groups are involved. The use of binoculars, spotting scopes or telephoto lenses will help when viewing small or distant animals.

The bushy-tailed woodrat, commonly called the "packrat," is rarely seen, but its massive nests of sticks and droppings are often easy to spot on rocky ledges.
Nancy Bostick-Ebbert

Ron Stewart

However, not all wildlife is easily observable from the road. For those whose time and abilities permit, there are great advantages to viewing wildlife in a more remote and natural setting. Even a short walk will increase your chances for viewing animals in their habitat. However, always be prepared for inclement weather, varied and often steep terrain, and of course for wild animals themselves. Look carefully for animal signs, such as footprints in mud or around water, twig nests up in the crevices of cliff-faces, scat (dung), pellets (indigestible material regurgitated by a bird of prey), or broken branches and twigs, which often indicate use of the area by deer, elk, or moose.

3. Listen for vocalizations. Many smaller mammals and birds would be virtually undetectable if not for their sounds, such as the scolding chatter of squirrels or the flute-like call of the hermit thrush. During certain seasons, sound may be the best way to "view" some wildlife species, such as elk, when the bulls can be heard bugling their challenges to each other during the fall rut (mating season). Vocalizations can provide such valuable information that certain population surveys are based upon it. For instance, because owls are nocturnal predators, their presence is virtually undetectable; therefore, biologists must rely on their calls in response to recorded vocalizations.

4. Patience may be a virtue, but for those who wish to observe wildlife, it is a necessity. The saying every child repeats when learning to cross the street—"Stop,

Great horned owl
Ron Stewart

Look, and Listen"—applies equally to wildlife viewing. Stop and wait at the edge of a meadow or clearing, look carefully before entering, and listen for vocalizations or sounds of movement. Sometimes, the best way to observe wildlife, especially birds, is to let them come to you. Find a comfortable site and begin making soft, repetitive "pish-pish" noises, which may provoke curious birds to investigate.

5. Finally, be respectful and ethical. Wildlife is just that—wild life. Never treat them as domesticated animals, a mistake some people will not have the opportunity to make twice! Carefully watch their behavior, and back away immediately if you see it change. Never approach mothers with young, or animals during the rut. Even deer have been known to turn aggressive during this time.

Remember that wild animals have specific diets, and human food is not on the menu. Be careful not to leave food or trash behind if you stop to eat. Some animals,

Mountain bluebird
Ron Stewart

such as bears, may become aggressive if fed by people, even unintentionally by dropping a scrap or leaving food outside in campsites. A fed bear is a dead bear!

The harassment of wildlife is a violation of state and federal laws and it is important to report any instances of such.

Perhaps in short, our relationship with the wild creatures should follow the old axiom, "Do unto others as you would have them do unto you," even if the "others" turn out to have four legs, feathers, or fur.

WILDLIFE FUN FACTS

Rocky Mountain Mule Deer (*Odocoileus hemionus*)
The Rocky Mountain mule deer is the most abundant large mammal species found along the Byway and throughout Utah. Named for their large ears, mule deer differ in both looks and behavior from their blacktail cousins of the west coast and the whitetail deer of eastern and central North America. Mule deer possess a unique way of escaping their predators, known as stotting. Instead of running, the "muley" will use all four legs like pogo sticks, jumping straight into the air. This

Ron Stewart

type of movement expends little energy and allows the deer to go over brush or other obstacles, traveling in a straight line while the predator is slowed down by having to go around.

Ron Stewart

Rocky Mountain Elk (*Cervus canadensis*)

Also known by its Shawnee name, "wapti," this large member of the deer family is related to the red deer of Eurasia. The ancestors of the North American species came across Beringia (the prehistoric land bridge between Alaska and Russia) during one or more of the past ice ages. There are several subspecies, one of which is extinct. Listen for bulls bugling during the rut (breeding season), from late August through early October.

Ron Stewart

Moose (*Alces alces shirasi*)

The name "moose" comes from an Algonquin word meaning "eater of twigs" and refers to the browsing habits of this largest member of the deer family. "Moose" is a strictly North American term; in Europe, this animal is called "elk." With long legs and spreading hooves, moose are well adapted to feeding in wet, marshy areas. Moose are solitary animals with associations formed only between a cow and her offspring. Even as big as it is, the "Shiras moose" subspecies of this region averages smaller than its Alaskan relatives. An Alaskan bull moose may weigh up to 1,600 pounds and stand 7.5 feet at the shoulder.

Pronghorn (*Antilocapra americana*)

Erroneously called an antelope, the pronghorn is the only surviving member of an otherwise extinct family of animals that were both numerous and diverse in the Miocene Epoch. Scientists have long puzzled over the blazing speed of the pronghorn, which can achieve bursts of sixty miles per hour, making it the second-fastest land animal in the world. Running at even half of their potential speed, pronghorns can easily outdistance any of their living predators. Why then develop an adaptation that is not necessary? The mystery was explained when a fossil species of cheetah, the world's fastest land animal, was discovered in North America.

Linda West

Ron Stewart

Ron Stewart/Courtesy UDWR

Ron Stewart/Courtesy UDWR

Rocky Mountain Bighorn Sheep (*Ovis canadensis*)

These wild sheep utilize a variety of habitats from mountain to desert. With their short, powerful legs and stocky bodies, bighorns escape their predators by climbing steep, rocky cliffs. Although they are social animals, rams and ewes generally live in separate herds until the rut, which occurs from late November through December. Bighorn rams have an intense and unusual method of fighting. Two dominant rams will approach and try to intimidate each other. If this fails, they rear up on their hind legs and lunge, battering each other with their horns. The effect is the same as running headlong into a brick wall at twenty miles per hour. Bony struts support the thickened skull, allowing the rams to clash without injury.

Ron Stewart

Coyote (*Canis latrans*)

The coyote's range includes parts of Canada, Mexico, Central America, and most of the United States. Showing amazing adaptation to many environments, they seem equally at home in city, farm, or desert. Known as "God's Dog" to the Dine (Navajo) people of the American Southwest, the coyote is a favorite, often mischievous, subject of many Native American stories. Generations of children learned many valuable lessons by listening to the exploits of "Coyote the Trickster" at the knees of their elders. Listen for the howls of coyotes in the low country around Steinaker and Red Fleet at night.

Mary Beth Bennis-Smith/Courtesy UFNH

Bats

Eighteen different species of bat live in Utah; two are known to hibernate in the bat cave located near the Sheep Creek Geologic loop. These include the Townsend's big-eared bat (*Corynorhinus townsendii*) and the Western small-footed bat (*Myotis ciliolabrum*). Both species prefer more open spaces than rock crevices for hibernating, making caves or mine shafts an ideal habitat. Since both species, particularly the Townsend's, are sensitive to disturbance during hibernation, the cave is closed from approximately October 1 through April 1. For information on cave access at other times, contact the Flaming Gorge Ranger District office in Manila. **Caving can be a dangerous activity and prior experience or a guide is required before entering the cave.**

Golden-mantled Ground Squirrel (*Spermophilus lateralis*)

Many people confuse these common rodents with chipmunks, and though both belong to the squirrel family, there are significant differences between them. The golden-mantled ground squirrel is larger and lacks the chipmunk's distinctive white eye stripe. These animals have an enviable life, filled with eating and breeding during the spring and summer months and sleeping for most of the rest of the year. The genus name, *Spermophilus*, means "seed lover," and seeds are a mainstay of their diet along with nuts, fungus, insects, berries, and even carrion (dead animals). During the summer, you may often see them with stuffed cheek pouches as they cache food for the long winter ahead.

Linda West

Ron Stewart

Yellow-bellied Marmot (*Marmota flaviventris*)

These large rodents are commonly seen in the middle to high elevations along the Byway in the spring and summer. Sometimes called "rock chucks," they prefer rocky outcroppings near meadows where they excavate multi-chambered burrows and live in small colonies. A large male may live with two to four females and their young. A female matures at age two and may have a litter of up to six young per year. If you hear a whistle, it may be a yellow-bellied marmot, as they use six different whistle sounds for everything from warning "Dangerous predator!" to locating their adventurous youngsters.

Chipmunks (*Tamias* species)

Several species of chipmunks occur along the Byway. They can be very difficult to tell apart, with subtle differences in color, size, and behavior, but all are easily distinguished from their cousin, the golden-mantled ground squirrel, by their small size and bold white eye stripes. The distinctive black stripes down the back are the subject of many Native American stories where the little animal barely escapes the sharp claws of a pursuing predator and is eternally marked. The ever-busy chipmunk spends the spring and summer months gathering food for its winter cache. During hibernation it will frequently rouse to eat from its food stores.

Rabbits and Hares

The Byway is a transition area for rabbits and hares. Five species—two cottontail rabbits (*Sylvilagus* species), two jackrabbits (actually hares, *Lepus* species) and the snowshoe hare (*Lepus americanus*)—are separated by elevation and community type. Desert cottontails are generally found in desert shrub below 6,000 feet, and mountain cottontails in the plant communities above. Similarly, black-tailed jackrabbits are common at low elevations on the south slope of the Uintas, and white-tailed jackrabbits at middle elevations on the north slope of the range. The desert-adapted black-tail has huge ears to shed heat, while the snow-adapted white-tail changes its brownish-gray summer fur to white during the winter, as does the snowshoe hare of the higher, forested elevations.

Longer legs and huge ears distinguish the black-tailed jackrabbit (left) from the desert cottontail (above).
Ron Stewart

Bears

Utah was once home to at least three species of bears: the giant short-faced bear, the grizzly or brown bear, and the American black bear. The short-faced bear was the largest predator known in North America, standing at roughly 5.5 feet at the shoulder. No chance of seeing one, though; it became extinct before the end of the last ice age. However, the grizzly survived in Utah until 1923, when the last of these bears was taken by a hunter.

Today only the much smaller black bear (*Ursus americanus*) remains. An average black bear is twenty-eight to thirty-two inches at the shoulder and males weigh 180 to 350 pounds. While most black bears are black, their fur can come in a range of colors from almost white to blonde, cinnamon, and chocolate brown. Like humans, their hair can even change color as they get older.

Ron Stewart

Surprisingly, considering their reputations, generally only a small part of their diet is meat, and most of that is winter-kills or animals killed by other natural or human causes. Studies show that roughly 70 to 80 percent of their food is plants, and the rest is insects and other invertebrates, small mammals, amphibians, reptiles, and fish.

Black bears can be found along the entire Byway, but most sightings are in the denser, forested areas. Unfortunately, bears find human foods, including pet foods and garbage, especially enticing. With their excellent sense of smell, they can be attracted into human camps and summer homes from miles away. Bears are smart and can quickly learn to associate humans or human structures with food. Once one does, it becomes a threat and has to be killed. **Don't force a wildlife manager to kill a bear just because you wanted a closer look or left food scraps on the table. Simply put, a fed bear is a dead bear, whether you had good intentions or not.**

River Otter (*Lontra canadensis*)

The playful river otter once more makes its home in the lakes and streams along the Byway. Between 1989 and 1992, the Utah Division of Wildlife Resources reintroduced sixty-seven otters from Alaska and Nevada into the Green River. From there, they have spread through Flaming Gorge Reservoir and up many of the tributary streams into the Uinta Mountains.

With webbed feet, sleek bodies, and rudder-like tails, otters are highly adapted to swimming. They are opportunistic foragers feeding mainly on fish, crayfish, and amphibians. However, they will take other mammals and birds if the opportunity presents itself. While otters are capable of catching trout, studies along the Green River indicate they feed primarily on crayfish, and the slower fish like carp and suckers. They have also been observed cleaning up dead or injured fish.

Another adaptation protects them underwater and from the winter cold. Their thick, waterproof fur traps air, adding insulation. Their fur was also their downfall. It was so highly prized that the early trappers nearly eliminated otters from the western states, including Utah.

The lucky visitor may find otters along the Green River, larger mountain streams, lakes, and the reservoir near submerged trees, log jams, rock piles, and beaver dams. Often, they can be seen sunning on a rock or a log. They may be seen swimming with just their heads out of the water or occasionally jumping out like small porpoises.

Eagles

Eagles are commonly seen perched on trees or power poles, or flying above the Byway. The golden eagle (*Aquila chrysaetos*), a year-round resident, is an excellent hunter of rabbits and other small mammals. The bald eagle (*Haliaeetus leucocephalus*) is mainly a winter visitor, although recently a few pairs have nested in the Uinta Basin area. During the summer, they are mainly fish eaters, but they also hunt ducks and small mammals, or scavenge. With an abundance of roadkills, and with ducks concentrated on a few open waters, Utah hosts one of the largest wintering populations of bald eagles. The best areas to view both species are the ends of the Byway, at Lucerne Bay near Manila, and around Steinaker Reservoir near Vernal.

Ron Stewart

Ron Stewart

Osprey (*Pandion haliaetus*)

With several adaptations, from its wing tips to the soles of its big feet, the osprey is a fish-catching expert. This "fish hawk" plunges into the water to catch fish, unlike bald eagles, which just snag fish off the surface. From spring through fall, ospreys might be seen near any of the lakes and reservoirs along the Byway, but one of the best places to look for them is near Flaming Gorge Dam, where several pairs have built large stick nests on rock pinnacles overlooking the reservoir. The birds are readily visible as they perch, catch fish, and raise their young.

Turkey Vulture (*Cathartes aura*)

Part of nature's "clean-up crew," turkey vultures are colonial nesters with established rookeries in the cliffs lining Flaming Gorge Reservoir. Vultures use thermals (rising warm air currents) to soar above the landscape, looking for roadkills or any dead animals. You may spot high-circling vultures almost anywhere along the Byway, but from the Red Canyon Visitor Center and rim trails you might see them up close, nearly at eye level.

Ron Stewart/Courtesy UDWR

Ron Stewart

Linda West

Corvids

A bird family well represented along the Byway is the corvids. This family includes the black-billed magpie, American crow, common raven, Clark's nutcracker, and various jays. Although not as large a family by sheer number of species as others in the area, the corvids are well known due to their large size, colorful or dramatic plumage, and in-your-face attitude; shy, they are not. They can be seen in all of the different ecosystems represented along the Byway, from the desert shrub community through the spruce-fir forests.

The scrub jay (above) mainly lives at lower elevations among shrubs and junipers, but the black-billed magpie (left) can be seen almost anywhere along the Byway.

Reptiles

Many different species of snakes and lizards live along the Scenic Byway, from the desert scrub up through the higher mountain meadows. Reptiles are known as ectotherms, meaning that their internal temperature closely reflects that of their environmental. Behavior—sunning when cool, seeking shade when warm—thus plays a large part in maintaining a steady temperature. The advantage to this type of metabolism is a much lower caloric intake compared to mammals, which are endotherms or self-regulating.

Although all lizards and snakes can bite, the rattlesnake is the only venomous reptile in the area. Be aware, not afraid, when in rattlesnake country. Never put your hands or feet in spaces that you cannot clearly see into, such as ledges above you, or in shaded areas under rocks. Wearing thick leather boots that extend up your calf is also recommended when hiking.

The gopher or bull snake (*Pituophis catenifer deserticola*), recognized by bold, squarish dark brown or black spots on a light tan background, is the snake that you are most likely to see along the Byway. Commonly reaching lengths of three or four feet, it eats mainly rodents, which it kills by constriction (coiling tightly around the prey until it suffocates). Although harmless to humans, if cornered it may try to scare off the threat by puffing up and hissing loudly, hence its nickname, "blow snake."

(Above left) Sagebrush lizard
Ron Stewart

(Above right) The gopher snake literally unhinges its jaws to swallow its prey whole.
Linda West

Ron Stewart

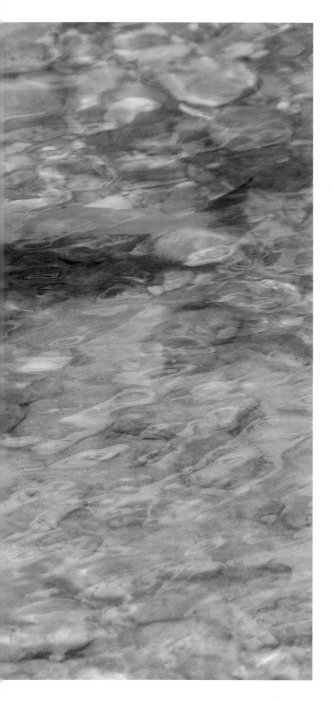

Kokanee Salmon
(*Oncorhynchus nerka*)
Sheep Creek, a tributary of Flaming Gorge, is one of the best places in the state to view salmon as they swim upriver to spawn from late August through September. The breeding fish become a brilliant red color, making them easy to spot. The Kokanee is a landlocked subspecies of the sockeye salmon, and was first introduced into Flaming Gorge in 1963. During the spawn, Sheep Creek is closed to fishing (please see the Utah Fishing Proclamation or contact the Division of Wildlife Resources for more information).

Ron Stewart/Courtesy UDWR

Colorado River Cutthroat Trout (*Oncorhynchus clarkii pleuriticus*)

The Colorado River cutthroat trout (CRCT) is the only trout native to the Uinta Mountains. Wildlife managers once believed this species was going extinct due to habitat loss and hybridization with introduced rainbow trout, but further investigations found a few genetically pure populations in remote streams in the Uinta Mountains. Captive breeding populations were established, and now CRCT are being produced in Utah's hatchery system and have been reintroduced into numerous waters.

A Sanctuary for Biodiversity

Along the Byway, it is possible to see some very rare and unusual species of wildlife. For example, the bald eagle and peregrine falcon were both recently delisted from the Threatened and Endangered Species list. Roughly half of Utah's "sensitive species" find safe refuge here.

The eastern Uinta Mountains, including Flaming Gorge Reservoir and the Green River, are a sanctuary because so much of the region is lightly developed. Also, biologists from the Utah Division of Wildlife Resources, U.S. Forest Service, and Bureau of Land Management have been aggressively trying to restore habitats in this area to a more natural succession of communities with an increased diversity of plant species.

Unfortunately, all of this can change with a few strokes of a pen. History shows that civilizations tend to devour natural lands to bring housing, energy, and other resources to fuel the growth of cities and other human developments.

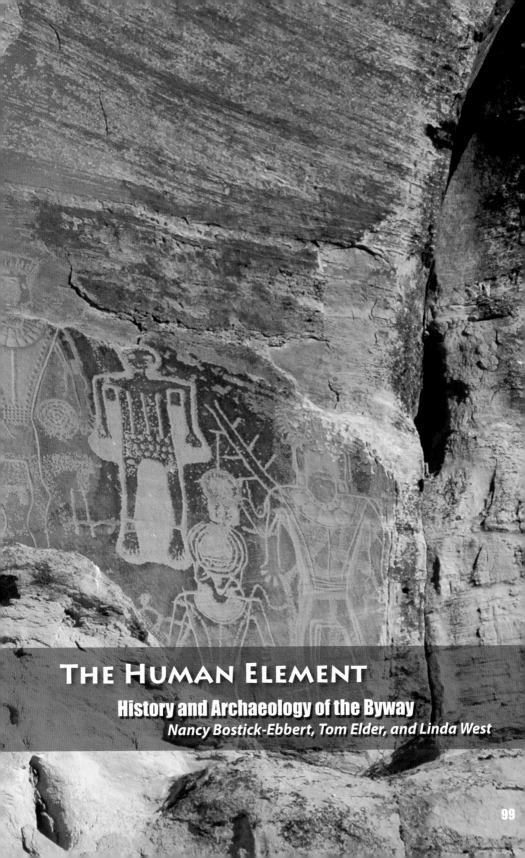

THE HUMAN ELEMENT

History and Archaeology of the Byway

Nancy Bostick-Ebbert, Tom Elder, and Linda West

Throughout human existence, people have settled in areas where water, food, and shelter were available. This is as true in northeastern Utah as anywhere else, but the rugged terrain, scarce water, and climatic extremes limited human travel and settlement well into modern times. No doubt many people have passed through the region over the millennia, and as you travel the Scenic Byway, you may be following or crossing routes that have been used for thousands of years. But until the last few centuries, we have discovered little evidence left by these visitors or residents. We are heir to a priceless, but often mysterious, cultural heritage.

THE EARLIEST PEOPLE

People have lived in this region for about 10,000 years or more. Designated as the Paleoindian and Archaic cultures by archaeologists, these early people depended almost entirely on hunting and gathering. Animals ranging from small rodents and rabbits to deer, bison, and bighorn sheep supplied protein, and many wild plants provided grains, berries, and nuts. For shelter, both cultures probably utilized natural rock overhangs when available, or built simple brush structures in more open areas. Because the people moved frequently with the seasons and according to the availability of plant and animal food, their material possessions were few and they left scant evidence behind. Throughout much of this time, particularly the earlier Paleoindian era, we have few clues other than stone projectile points, some of which were found along Red Canyon and near Dutch John.

Excavations around Dutch John have produced better evidence of lengthy Archaic occupation, beginning as far back as 8,000 years ago. Firepits there yielded organic material such as charcoal and bone that can be carbon-dated, and the Dutch John area may have been used for thousands of years as a seasonal base, especially in summer and fall, for wider hunting and foraging.

Archaic hunters had long used the atlatl, a throwing stick that increases the range and force of a spear. By around the time of Christ, they were also adopting new technologies such as the bow and arrow, and beginning to cultivate a few plants. Together, these changes led to a more settled lifestyle and the accumulation of more material goods such as various bone and stone tools, woven sandals, and coiled basketry. At some point, these trends produced northeastern Utah's best known prehistoric culture, the Fremont.

Both Archaic and Fremont hunters used the atlatl (the shorter stick underneath the spear). Its extra leverage gave a thrown spear greater distance and force.
Linda West/Courtesy INHA

THE FREMONT CULTURE

Most archaeologists believe that the Fremont Culture developed from the Archaic hunter-gatherers of the Colorado Plateau and eastern Great Basin. Originally living in small, highly mobile bands, the predecessors of the Fremont began to settle and multiply where resources permitted. Not surprisingly in this arid land, a reliable water supply usually dictated such sites. The Fremont Culture was named for the Fremont River in south-central Utah, where archaeologists first studied it. The culture has since been traced through much of Utah (chiefly west and north of the Colorado River) and parts of Nevada, Idaho, Colorado, and Wyoming.

Like later immigrants of both Native American and European descent, the Fremont people found the Uinta Basin a welcoming place to live. The northern edge of the basin had many desirable resources within a relatively small area. Ashley Creek, Brush Creek, and others fed by Uinta Mountain snows provided fish, waterfowl, and numerous mammals attracted to the streamside greenery. Many types of plants including grasses, forbs, marsh plants, and berries were readily available. Then as now, pinyon-juniper woodlands covered the lower hills and provided a favored winter settlement location, while the higher elevations of the Uintas offered an excellent subsistence strategy for warmer months. Beyond the mountains, the high plains of Wyoming provided hunters with a wide array of game, such as bison and pronghorn.

Wild game and plants remained important in their diet, but as early as about 1 A.D., the Fremont people began to cultivate maize (corn), and later added beans and squash. It appears that the regional climate 2,000 years ago was somewhat milder and wetter than at present, which encouraged the development of small, scattered farmsteads. Steinaker Gap, a site discovered in 1992 when the Bureau of Reclamation began work to reinforce Steinaker Dam, appears to have been such a farmstead.

When, around 500 A.D., the climate began to change, periods of drought probably forced the Fremont population to

Corn was a staple of the Fremont diet. Linda West/Courtesy INHA

concentrate in villages near the most reliable streams, such as Brush Creek near the Byway and Cub Creek a few miles east in Dinosaur National Monument. Their dwellings were often pithouses, which were partially dug into the ground, rimmed with low rock walls, and roofed with branches and mud. Where natural

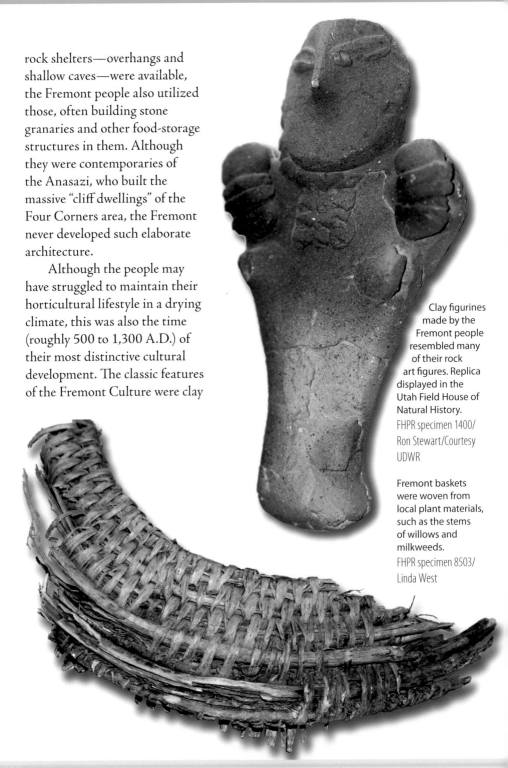

rock shelters—overhangs and shallow caves—were available, the Fremont people also utilized those, often building stone granaries and other food-storage structures in them. Although they were contemporaries of the Anasazi, who built the massive "cliff dwellings" of the Four Corners area, the Fremont never developed such elaborate architecture.

Although the people may have struggled to maintain their horticultural lifestyle in a drying climate, this was also the time (roughly 500 to 1,300 A.D.) of their most distinctive cultural development. The classic features of the Fremont Culture were clay

Clay figurines made by the Fremont people resembled many of their rock art figures. Replica displayed in the Utah Field House of Natural History. FHPR specimen 1400/ Ron Stewart/Courtesy UDWR

Fremont baskets were woven from local plant materials, such as the stems of willows and milkweeds. FHPR specimen 8503/ Linda West

FHPR specimen 1397/Ron Stewart/Courtesy UDWR

trapezoidal figurines adorned with necklaces and blunt hairstyles; an unusual one-rod-and-bundle basketry style; thin-walled gray pottery; hide moccasins with heels formed by the dew claws of deer or bighorn sheep; and above all, spectacular rock art scattered on soaring cliffs, rock slabs, and boulders throughout the region.

The art of this "wilderness Louvre," as it has been called, consists of both petroglyphs and pictographs. Petroglyphs are designs that were carved or pecked into rock using stone or bone tools. Pictographs were painted on with mineral or organic pigments. Being much more fragile, pictographs have survived to the present mainly in sheltered sites such as caves and overhangs. Many petroglyphs likely also included painted areas that have weathered away.

Fremont rock art features geometric designs such as zigzags, concentric circles, and spirals; animals, especially bighorn sheep but also deer, mountain lions, dogs or coyotes, snakes, and lizards; and stylized human figures called anthropomorphs. These typically have trapezoidal bodies with broad shoulders and narrow waists, and heads that may feature horns and/or earrings. In Uinta Basin rock art sites, the anthropomorphs are often elaborately adorned—with headdresses, necklaces,

loincloths, and shields—in what is called the Classic Vernal Style. The best examples of these can be seen in Dry Fork Canyon, a few miles west of Vernal. Dinosaur National Monument also has major sites at McKee Spring, Jones Hole, and Cub Creek.

Only two petroglyph panels can be seen on the Byway itself. Both are near the crossing of Big Brush Creek, and unfortunately, they have been badly vandalized. Most people are not so thoughtless, but wherever you see rock art, please do not touch it, since even slight pressure and skin oils can damage it.

Though the Fremont lifestyle served them well for centuries, sometime between 1,200 and 1,300 A.D. their world began to crumble, and most of the traits that characterized the Fremont Culture simply vanished. An increasingly dry climate, with longer and more severe droughts, seems to have ended Fremont horticulture in the Uinta Basin. Peripheral groups along the Green River in Red Canyon and Browns Park managed to survive until 1,550 A.D. or later, through a combination of corn-growing in the bottomlands and hunting and gathering in the higher elevations, but eventually, they too disappeared. There is little evidence to indicate whether these people died out, migrated elsewhere, or were absorbed or killed by other hunter-gatherer societies.

(Opposite) Elaborately decorated anthropomorphs, like these in Dry Fork Canyon, typify the "Classic Vernal Style" of Fremont rock art. (Also see page 96.)
Nancy Bostick-Ebbert

(Below) Fremont pictographs on a sheltered cliff at Jones Hole portray bighorn sheep, an important source of meat and hides for the ancient people.
Nancy Bostick-Ebbert

One thing is clear: the Fremont people were hardy and innovative, and their ability to interpret the world around them showed an artistic vision of lasting beauty. The unique petroglyphs and pictographs of northeastern Utah are a tangible reminder of a people long since vanished.

THE UTES

When Europeans began to enter the American West, among the native peoples they encountered were the Noochew ("The People," their name for themselves), or Utes. Occupying much of modern Utah (derived from the name Ute, which means "high places" or "close to the sun") and Colorado, the Noochew were comprised of twelve distinct bands that traded and intermarried with each other, but were not dominated by a larger tribal organization. Before they acquired horses, each band controlled only as much area as it could travel on foot, and each respected the traditional boundaries of the others' home territories. What is now northeastern Utah was home to the Yoowetuh or Uinta-at ("lodgepole pine") band.

The Noochew practiced a free-ranging subsistence lifestyle that made the best use of their environment, with extended family groups of twenty to one hundred people moving through hunting and gathering territories as the seasons dictated. They hunted large and small game with bows and arrows, nets, and spears, and harvested many kinds of seeds, berries, roots, pine nuts, and herbs to round out their diets. Where good pine poles were available—as in the lodgepole forests of the Uintas—they lived in hide-covered tipis. In other areas, brush lean-to shelters, layered and packed with mud insulation, were used.

The Noochew were renowned for their beautiful brain-tanned buckskins and woven willow water jugs, sealed with pine pitch to make them waterproof. Both the buckskins and water jugs were prized and highly sought after by many tribes, and the Utes traded them to obtain other needed goods.

Locally, the Uinta-at band maintained ties with their Shoshone relatives to the north, and followed about the same route as U.S. Highway 191 when traveling to visit them. The valley now filled by Steinaker Reservoir was a resting place on the journey, and a few miles farther along, the Red Fleet rock formations are still considered a power location, sacred to the Ute people. In the Flaming Gorge area, they stocked up on water, game, and berries for the long trek across the dry hills and plains of what is now southwestern Wyoming.

The horse came to the Utes via the Spanish in the 1600s. This increased their mobility, enhanced their big game hunting prowess, and enabled the Utes to perfect their skills as warriors, earning them a reputation as fierce raiders. However, later changes brought by people of European descent would prove more difficult for the Noochew to adapt to.

The Noochew Creation Story

As told by Larry Cesspooch

Sinauf, the Creator, half man and half wolf, was breaking off sticks, all sizes, from the trees and placing them in a large bag. He did this for a long time, as he was preparing for a long journey to the North. Meanwhile, curious Coyote was watching as Sinauf did this.

When the Creator went off to rest, Coyote snuck over to peek in the magic bag. He heard all kinds of noises coming from the bag; this made him even more curious. Coyote opened the bag to find Human Beings of all kinds, speaking different languages. When all the people began to crawl out of the bag, Coyote tried to put them back in, but there were too many, so he panicked and ran away.

When Sinauf returned, he found the bag open and all the people gone, except one group. The Creator reached into the bag and gently pulled them out, saying, "My Children, I will call you Utikas." He then placed them high in the mountains to be close to him.

Sinauf told them: "You will be brave and strong and able to defeat all the rest." Then, he sang a special song as he placed them in the Rocky Mountains of Colorado and the Uinta and Wasatch Mountains of Utah.

Sinauf had intended to distribute all the Human Beings evenly throughout Mother Earth, but because Coyote released them, human beings now fight over land and religion. For his mischievous deed, the Creator told Coyote: "From now on, you will cry every night to the moon for what you did."

Because of their Creation Story, the Noochew believe they have always lived in the mountains of Utah and Colorado. They acknowledge that archaeologists and anthropologists say the Anasazi and Fremont Cultures preceded the Utes, but they feel those were simply their own people who grew and developed to become who they are today.

Ute elders also say that "rock writing" (not "rock art" as it is called by archaeologists) is derived from the universal sign language that made it possible for native tribes to communicate with each other. The Ute people believe that the storytellers who left these messages on the rocks received spiritual instruction on what to say and where to place it. Rock writing, they say, is important (indicated by the effort taken to make it so durable) and sacred, and harm will come to those who disturb it.

Acquisition of horses increased the Utes' mobility and made them formidable hunters and raiders. Rock art replica displayed in Utah Field House of Natural History.
Ron Stewart/Courtesy UDWR

In a pattern familiar throughout the West, as pioneers arrived and cleared forests to build homes and plant crops, the native people lost their traditional hunting grounds and other food sources, and conflicts were inevitable. In 1861, President Lincoln set aside 2 million acres in the Uinta Basin as a reservation for the Utes. Unwilling to adopt a settled, agrarian life, they resisted in a series of attacks and raids known as the Black Hawk War. After five years that left many of them starving, the Uinta-at band relented and traveled to the reservation.

Similar conflicts with settlers and prospectors in Colorado led to the relocation of additional Ute bands to the enlarged Uintah-Ouray Reservation in the 1880s. However, in the next two decades, the federal government "allotted" the reservation lands, giving each Ute 80 to 160 acres for farming, plus access to a communal grazing district. The rest of the "reservation" land was opened for white settlers.

In the 1930s, the Utes of the Uintah and Ouray Reservation formed a business council and incorporated as the Northern Ute Tribe—the governing body that remains intact today. Revenues from the Central Utah Project (water storage) and energy development (oil and natural gas) have helped Ute families survive, but unemployment and poverty remain serious challenges. In 1986, the U.S. Supreme Court upheld the tribe's longstanding contention that it had the right to exercise legal jurisdiction over all pre-allotment reservation lands. While having no immediate impact on area residents, this ruling is an important symbol for the Ute people, and highlights their desire to establish their rightful place as a political entity.

The Northern Ute Tribe now has an enrollment of over 3,000 members who have taken many steps to preserve their cultural traditions and native language while working to improve their economic circumstances through various enterprises, educational opportunities, and planned economic development. Each year, the tribe hosts pow-wows, the Sun Dance, the Bear Dance, rodeos, and other events, celebrating their own heritage and allowing non-Indians an opportunity to learn more about Utah's first Americans.

Ute rock art and historical records indicate that bison once roamed in the Uinta Basin. Replica displayed in Utah Field House of Natural History.
Ron Stewart/Courtesy UDWR

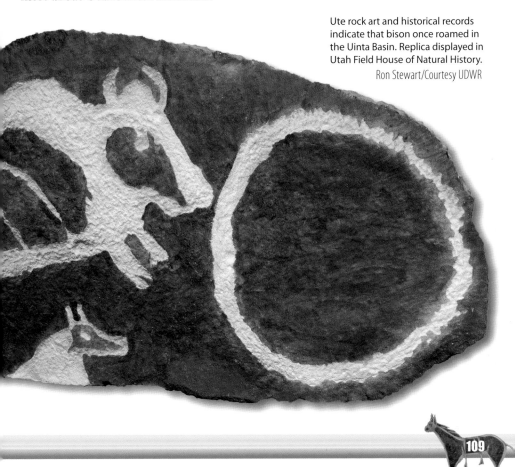

Dancers in colorful garb perform at modern Ute pow-wows.
Nancy Bostick-Ebbert

How Do You Spell That?

Throughout this book, you will see a name derived from that of the local Ute band. However, you may have noticed that it is sometimes spelled "Uinta," and sometimes "Uintah." Both spellings are correct, but the usual standard is to apply the former to geologic and geographic features (Uinta Mountains, Uinta Basin) and the latter to cultural entities (Uintah County, Uintah-Ouray Reservation). It is not a hard and fast rule; Wyoming, for instance, has a Uinta County.

MODERN HISTORY

Even in recent times, the region traversed by the Scenic Byway is not so much known for its colorful history, as for the lack of much known history. Massive gorges such as Big and Little Brush Creeks, and of course Flaming Gorge and Red Canyon on the Green River, prevented easy access until the late twentieth century. Despite a thriving folklore about "lost" mines and hidden Spanish treasure, no spectacular discoveries led to silver or gold rushes, such as happened in many other places. The most exciting scientific explorations took place in the canyons of the Green River off to the east and south.

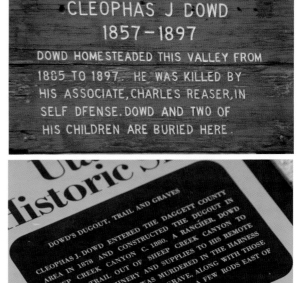

Discrepancies between two signs near the grave of Cleophas Dowd in Sheep Creek Canyon illustrate how the details of history are often lost through the years. Linda West

Of course, many "common" people lived and died here. Their lives were sometimes long and peaceful, and sometimes cut short by illness, accidents, or outlawry; all no doubt rich in personal significance, but rarely famous. Take, for example, the man who is buried on the Sheep Creek Geological Loop. In the course of a turbulent life that seems to have included ordination as a Catholic priest, gun-slinging, appointment as a deputy sheriff, and supplying horses to outlaws, Cleophas J. Dowd homesteaded on Sheep Creek in the 1880s and was killed by a hired hand in 1897. Contradictory details on two signs near his grave serve to illustrate how even such an eventful life may remain shrouded in obscurity.

The following is a timeline of some of the most significant events that occurred along or near the Byway.

1776   Local written history began with the coming of the Dominguez-Escalante expedition. Seeking a route from Santa Fe, New Mexico, to the missions of California, these two padres crossed the Green River near the future Dinosaur National Monument Quarry site. Winter turned them back in the deserts of western Utah, and they returned to Santa Fe.

1825   With a small party of fur trappers, General William H. Ashley became the first known river runner of the Green, floating in buffalo-skin "bullboats" through Flaming Gorge and Red Canyon. He left the inscription "Ashley 1825" at Ashley Falls, now submerged by Flaming Gorge Reservoir. Abandoning the river somewhere below the creek that now bears his name, Ashley returned north and arranged the first rendezvous at Henrys Fork (near Manila). The rendezvous system—an annual, wild celebration at which trappers exchanged beaver pelts for trade goods—

continued for only fifteen years, but left a colorful mark that is still celebrated by modern-day "mountain man" rendezvous at nearby Fort Bridger, Wyoming, and many other places.

1861   Brigham Young, president of the Latter-Day Saints (LDS) Mormon church, sent an expedition to the Uinta Basin to determine its suitability for settlement. The report stated that the area was a "vast contiguity of waste... valueless excepting for nomadic purposes, hunting grounds for Indians and to hold the world together." (This unflattering description has not been perpetuated by modern chambers of commerce.) Nevertheless, a few ranchers began filtering into the basin over the next few decades.

1869   Major John Wesley Powell floated the canyons previously visited by Ashley, continuing on to the Colorado River and through the Grand Canyon. His account, *The Exploration of the Colorado River and Its Canyons*, remains a classic read. With poetic flair, Powell named many landmarks, such as Flaming Gorge, the Canyon of Lodore, and Split Mountain. He repeated most of the trip in 1871–1872 as one of the official government surveys of the West.

1869–1872   Two other federally sponsored scientific surveys visited the Uinta Mountain region. Ferdinand V. Hayden explored and mapped the northern slope of the Uintas in 1870, before going on to document the wonders of Wyoming's Yellowstone region. Clarence

The Scientists' Mountain Range

One unusual distinction of the Uinta Mountains is the scientific theme to the names of its major peaks. All of the major summits are named for distinguished geologists, a "who's who" of scientists who explored and mapped the West, including John Wesley Powell, Clarence King, Clarence Dutton, Ebenezer Emmons, Louis Agassiz, G. K. Gilbert, and Ferdinand V. Hayden.

The easternmost Uinta summits are Leidy Peak, Untermann Peak, and Marsh Peak. All three are occasionally visible from high points on the Byway. Leidy Peak, marking the eastern end of the "above-timberline" Uintas, was named for Joseph Leidy (1823–1891). Leidy assembled and described *Hadrosaurus*, a duckbilled dinosaur that was the first nearly complete skeleton of a dinosaur ever found.

To the west of Leidy, Untermann Peak is named for the father-and-son team of Ernest and G. E. Untermann. Ernest was the artist of the well-known paintings of prehistoric animals displayed at the Utah Field House of Natural History. His son, G. E. "Ernie" Untermann, was a geologist and served as the museum's first director.

Locally known as "Baldy," the only snow-capped peak visible from Vernal is officially named Marsh Peak, named after Othniel Charles Marsh (1831–1899). Marsh was a professor of vertebrate paleontology at Yale University, and named and described many well-known dinosaurs such as *Diplodocus longus* (closely related to "Dippy," the *Diplodocus carnegii* skeleton at the Field House) and *Allosaurus*, which later became Utah's state fossil.

Leidy Peak, on the skyline south of Red Canyon, is named for a prominent nineteenth-century paleontologist.
Linda West

King, later named the first director of the U.S. Geological Survey, mapped various parts of the Uintas in 1869 and 1871–1872. In the latter year, he exposed the infamous "Diamond Hoax" just north of Browns Park, where a pair of con men "salted" an area with gems and swindled wealthy investors by claiming that they had discovered a diamond mine.

1873 Captain Pardon Dodds built the first cabin in Ashley Valley, a few miles northwest of present Vernal.

1881 Fort Thornburgh, just northwest of present Vernal, was established to enforce the relocation of western Colorado Utes onto the nearby reservation. Over the next few years, a rough road known as the Carter Military Trail was built across the Uintas to connect the fort with Fort Bridger in southwestern Wyoming. The route chosen was too high and often closed in by snow and mud, but was still used into the 1920s, long after Fort Thornburgh's abandonment in 1884.

1890s Outlaws, including Butch Cassidy's Wild Bunch, frequently passed through or hid out in the rough Green River canyon country to the east, in particular at Browns Park.

1897 Vernal, which had been slowly growing through the 1870s and 1880s, was formally incorporated as a town. In the same year, President Grover Cleveland designated most of the Uinta Mountains as the Uinta Forest Reserve.

Sandstone for the Vernal Latter-Day Saints Tabernacle was quarried from this ridge across the highway and to the north of the Steinaker Nature Trail parking area. Ron Stewart/Courtesy UDWR

1901   The Latter-Day Saints Vernal Tabernacle (later rededicated as a temple) was built using rock quarried from the Frontier Sandstone. Near the turnoff to Steinaker Reservoir, an old wagon trail can be dimly seen rising up the side of the ridge east of the highway. Where one large sandstone boulder is perched on a prominent slump is the area from which the Mormon residents of Vernal blasted and levered off blocks of building stone.

1906   The Green brothers filed for a homestead in the area now called Greendale.

117

The Swett family established their ranch amid the meadows and craggy hills above Red Canyon. Now preserved as a historic site, the ranch is open to visitors from Memorial Day through Labor Day.
Ron Stewart/Courtesy UDWR

1908   President Teddy Roosevelt created the Ashley National Forest in the eastern Uinta Mountains, replacing part of the earlier Uinta Forest Reserve.

1909   Elizabeth Swett filed a homestead claim in Greendale, where her son Oscar had been grazing cattle. Oscar later filed adjoining claims, and with his wife Emma, developed an expansive ranching and logging operation, which they and their children operated mainly with horsepower clear into the 1960s. Swett Ranch is now a historic site within Flaming Gorge National Recreation Area.

1909   Earl Douglass of the Carnegie Museum of Natural History (Pittsburgh, Pennsylvania) discovered dinosaur fossils near Jensen, a few miles east of Vernal. In 1915, President Woodrow Wilson proclaimed the site as Dinosaur National Monument.

1915   Mining claims were filed on the Park City Formation where commercial quantities of phosphate were detected (large-scale mining did not begin until 1961).

1920s   An automobile road was constructed between Vernal and Daggett County, following about the same route as modern U.S. 191–Utah 44 and replacing the old Carter Military Trail.

1948   The Utah Field House of Natural History, designed to showcase local geology, paleontology, and history, opened in Vernal. Later incorporated into the Utah State Park

Established in 1948, the Utah Field House of Natural History moved to this new building in 2004. Jim Harland/ Courtesy Utah State Parks

system, it moved to a new building in 2004, and now serves as the southern portal of the Flaming Gorge-Uintas National Scenic Byway.

1958–1964 Flaming Gorge Dam was constructed as part of the Colorado River Storage Project (CRSP). The town of Dutch John was built to house and serve the dam's construction force, and the highway (now U.S. 191) between it and Vernal was improved during this time. The rising waters of Flaming Gorge Reservoir submerged the little town of Linwood, just east of Manila. Power generation at the dam began in 1963.

1959–1962   Steinaker Dam, a unit of the Central Utah Project (a participating project of the CRSP), was built to store water for release into the canals of Ashley Valley.

1965   Heavy rains caused a debris flow that raged down Sheep Creek Canyon on the night of June 9, killing a family of seven who were camped there. The site was designated as Palisades Memorial Park, now a picnic area on the Sheep Creek Geologic Loop.

1968   Flaming Gorge National Recreation Area was established.

1977   On July 16, the Cart Creek Fire killed three men who were trapped by wind-fanned flames. The men are honored with a plaque at the Firefighters Memorial Campground.

1980   Red Fleet Dam, another Central Utah Project unit, was built on Big Brush Creek, creating Red Fleet Reservoir.

1998   U.S. Highway 191 and Utah S.R. 44 were designated the Flaming Gorge-Uintas National Scenic Byway.

Flaming Gorge Dam
Doug Sprinkel

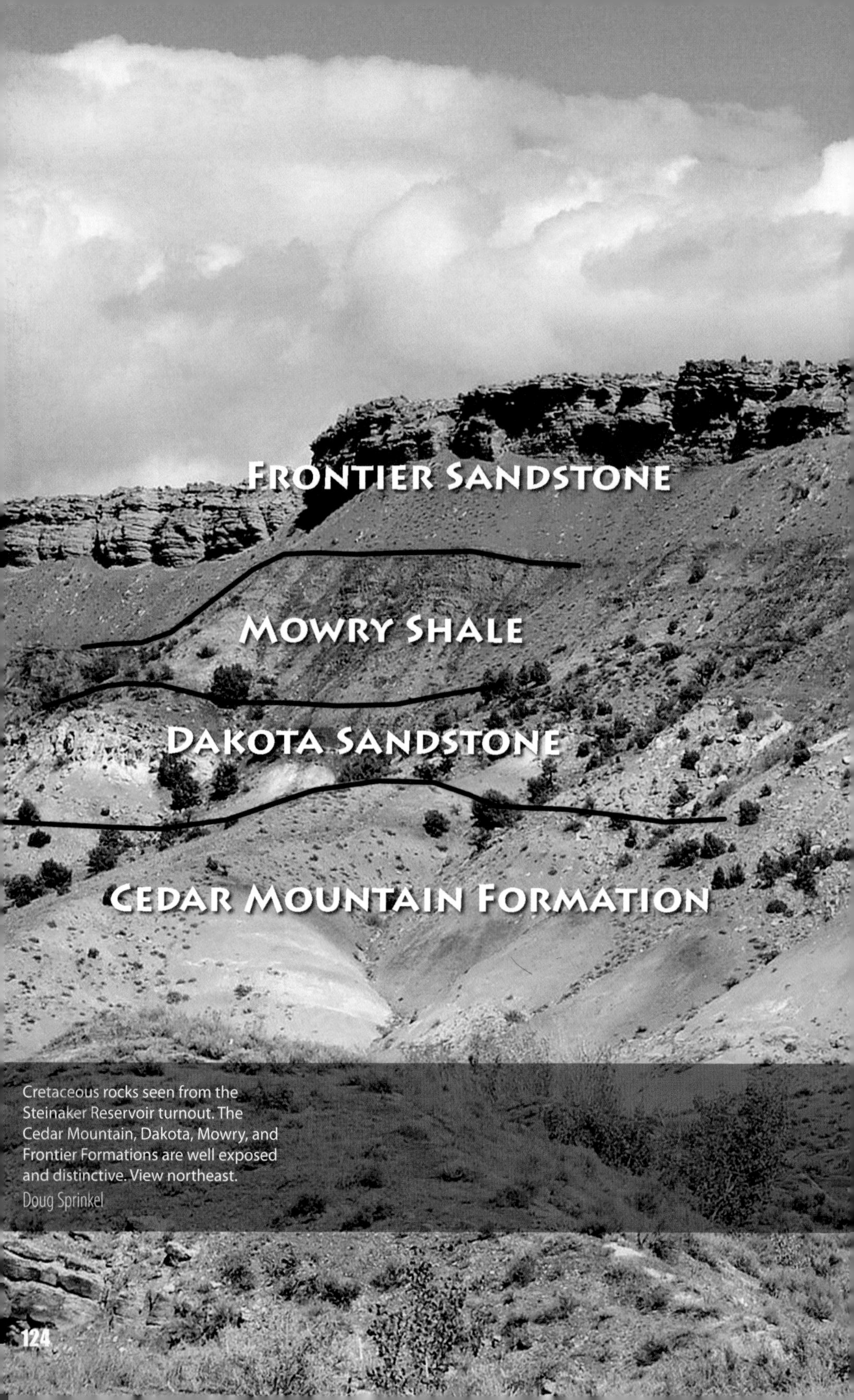

FRONTIER SANDSTONE

MOWRY SHALE

DAKOTA SANDSTONE

CEDAR MOUNTAIN FORMATION

Cretaceous rocks seen from the Steinaker Reservoir turnout. The Cedar Mountain, Dakota, Mowry, and Frontier Formations are well exposed and distinctive. View northeast.
Doug Sprinkel

ROAD LOGS

Mile-by-Mile Guide to the Byway
U.S. 191 and Utah S.R. 44-43

A NOTE ON GEOLOGIC NAMES USED IN THIS GUIDE

The naming of rock formations follows a specific set of rules outlined by the North American Commission on Stratigraphic Nomenclature in the North American Stratigraphic Code. The first part of the name refers to a geographic location where the rock unit was first or best described. The second part of the name indicates the dominant rock type such as sandstone or limestone; however, if the named rock unit contains several rock types the term "Formation" may be used. Sometimes, a named rock unit can be subdivided into discrete mappable units. These subunits are called "Members," such as the Gartra Member of the Chinle Formation. The second part of the name is also capitalized to indicate the named rock unit or subunit is formally recognized; lowercase is used to indicate informal use. In addition, research continues on many rock formations, which may result in a name change. At the time that this book was coming to publication, it became apparent that the geology signs along the Byway would be updated to reflect current geologic data. To accommodate these updates, the *Field Guide* will indicate first the correct, formally recognized name of the unit in question, and directly beside it in parentheses, the former name.

Most of the points in the road logs identify the various rock formations or other geologic phenomena; some also highlight plants, wildlife, or cultural features. Major points of interest are marked in the road log with the following icons:

B = Scenic Byway interpretive site

= geology

= wildlife viewing

= plant communities

= cultural (history/archaeology)

= nature trail

Many public and recreational facilities noted in the road logs have varying hours of operation according to the season. Most are open from at least the Memorial Day through Labor Day weekends; a few are open year-round, except for some holidays. Check directly with the managing agency for specific information.

U.S. HIGHWAY 191 SEGMENT

Road guide for the Flaming Gorge-Uintas National Scenic Byway, U.S. Highway 191 segment from Vernal to the Utah–Wyoming state line. The drive is a little more than fifty miles long but will likely take several hours depending on the number of stops the traveler makes along the way. The road guide is written to be driven north from Vernal, but can be started on the Utah–Wyoming state line and driven south.

Cumulative Miles (Incremental Miles) Icon(s)	Description

0.0 (0.0) **UTAH FIELD HOUSE OF NATURAL HISTORY STATE PARK MUSEUM**

The Utah Field House of Natural History was established in 1948 to preserve local geological, paleontological, and archaeological resources, and later became a Utah State Park. Now located at 496 East Main in Vernal, it also serves as an information center and as the southern portal of the Flaming Gorge-Uintas National Scenic Byway.

Set your trip odometer to zero and exit the parking lot onto 500 East and turn left. Turn left on Main Street (U.S. Highway 40) and travel west.

0.5 (0.5) Intersection of Main Street (U.S. Highway 40) and Vernal Avenue (U.S. Highway 191).

Turn right on Vernal Avenue (U.S. Highway 191) and travel north.

4.1 (3.6) **STOP**:

The "Drive Through the Ages" kiosk describes the general geology seen along the Scenic Byway. The kiosk is very near the formation boundary between the Mancos Shale and the underlying Frontier Sandstone. The Frontier is the sandstone hogback west of the highway; the Mancos Shale forms the vegetation-barren hills east of the highway. Note the relatively flat surface on top of the Mancos Shale. The surface is covered with gravel deposits that once formed the valley floor. Since the deposition of gravel, about 30,000 to 120,000 years ago, erosion cut down through the gravel and into the underlying soft Mancos Shale.

ARCHAEOLOGY:
Across the highway near the foot of Steinaker Dam, an archaeological site was discovered during reinforcement of the dam. Named Steinaker Gap, the site is believed to have been a Fremont Culture farmstead.
After stop, continue north on U.S. 191.

4.2 (0.1) **MANCOS SHALE (MANCOS FORMATION SIGN)**

4.4 (0.2) **FRONTIER SANDSTONE (FRONTIER FORMATION SIGN)**

4.5 (0.1) **MOWRY SHALE**
The silver-gray slopes are outcrops of Mowry Shale.

4.6 (0.1) **DAKOTA SANDSTONE**
The yellowish-gray sandstone belongs to the Dakota Sandstone.

4.7 (0.1) **STEINAKER RESERVOIR. STOP:**

The turnout on the left is a good place to view the succession of Jurassic and Cretaceous rocks. Steinaker Reservoir is west of the highway and fills the valley underlain mostly by the Jurassic Morrison Formation. The Morrison Formation is mostly covered by alluvium, where not underwater. Overlying the Morrison is the Cretaceous Cedar Mountain Formation, which is exposed along the shore here. East of the highway is a great view of the Dakota Sandstone (yellow-gray beds at road level), the Mowry Shale (the silver-gray slope), and the Frontier Sandstone (the yellowish-brown slope and sandstone that caps the ridge). See page 122.
WILDLIFE VIEWING #1
Elevation: 5,578 feet
Watch for ducks, geese, and loons on the water and shorebirds along the banks. Numerous songbirds can be found nesting in the cottonwood trees along the edge. Keep an eye out for osprey in the summer and bald eagles in the winter.
After stop, continue north on U.S. 191.

Ron Stewart

5.3 (0.5)   **CEDAR MOUNTAIN FORMATION**

5.7 (0.4)   **STEINAKER NATURE TRAIL. STOP:**
Displays here introduce the Scenic Byway's theme of "Wildlife

Through the Ages," and the short nature trail develops the theme further with the changing habitats through time that shape plant and animal communities. The nature trail is an excellent place to see many species of songbirds.

PLANTS:
Cottonwoods, willows, and other riparian (water-dependent) plants form a comparatively lush green band on the edges of Steinaker Reservoir, but a short distance beyond the high-water line, vegetation changes rapidly to the desert shrub community. Greasewood dominates the alkaline soil on the valley bottom here, and various other drought-tolerant species dot the hills. From

here on up to the Red Fleet area, many of these shrubs provide important winter forage.

HISTORY:

Remnants of an old wagon road and a quarry are visible on the hillside across the highway and to the north. Rock for the Vernal Latter-Day Saints Tabernacle/Temple was quarried from the Frontier Sandstone that caps the ridge.

After stop, continue north on U.S. 191.

6.0 (0.3)   **ENTRANCE TO STEINAKER STATE PARK**

Campground, boat ramp, and day-use areas are available; contact Utah State Parks for further information.

Continue north on U.S. 191, unless you are visiting the park.

7.1 (1.1)   **(OPTIONAL UNPAVED PULLOUT ON WEST)**

The pinkish-gray to light-brown rugged outcrops west of the highway are Nugget Sandstone. The low greenish hills in front of the Nugget Sandstone are beds of the Jurassic Stump Formation. As you continue up the Scenic Byway toward the Uinta Mountains, the brightly colored mudstones on the east/southeast side of the highway are Jurassic Morrison Formation, with Cretaceous Cedar Mountain through Frontier beds exposed in the upper part of the ridge; the resistant sandstone that caps the ridge is the upper part of the Frontier Sandstone.

Continue north on U.S. 191.

10.3 (3.2)   **(OPTIONAL UNPAVED PULLOUTS ON EAST OR WEST)**

The hogback ahead to the north is Jurassic Stump Formation with the Triassic–Jurassic Nugget Sandstone forming the dramatic pinkish-gray outcrops in the middle distance. The phosphate mine within the Permian Park City Formation can be seen on the distant slope. The ragged light-colored cliffs that form the upper part of the plateau above and to the left and right of the mine are beds of the Pennsylvanian–Permian Weber Sandstone. The Diamond Mountain Plateau is in view to the east and northeast, and the Yampa Plateau is in view to the southeast.

Continue north on U.S. 191.

10.4 (0.1)   STUMP FORMATION (CURTIS FORMATION SIGN)
Forty years ago, geologists thought this was the Curtis Formation, but additional research since then has demonstrated that only the lower sandstone is the Curtis Member, while the upper greenish shale and capping limestone are the Redwater Member, of the Stump Formation.

10.6 (0.2)   CARMEL FORMATION SIGN

10.7 (0.1)   ENTRANCE TO RED FLEET STATE PARK
Campground, boat ramp, and day-use areas are available; contact Utah State Parks for further information.
Continue north on U.S. 191, unless you are visiting the park.

11.0 (0.3)   NUGGET SANDSTONE (NAVAJO SANDSTONE SIGN)
This formation is now mapped as the Nugget Sandstone.

11.4 (0.4)   CHINLE AND GARTRA (SHINARUMP) FORMATION SIGNS
The conglomeratic sandstone that crops out near the signs is the basal member of the Chinle Formation, called the Gartra Member. Forty years ago, this unit was thought to be the Shinarump (a formal member of the Chinle Formation), which is well exposed in southern Utah and northern Arizona. However, intensive uranium exploration and additional research have shown that the Shinarump was not deposited this far north.

11.8 (0.4)   DINOSAUR TRACKWAY TRAIL JUNCTION
Optional side trip, 2.3 miles to trailhead parking; the hike to the trackways on the shore of Red Fleet Reservoir is about 2.5 miles round trip, best done in early morning or late afternoon in summer.
Continue north on U.S. 191, unless you are hiking the trail.

11.9 (0.1)   MOENKOPI FORMATION SIGN

12.3 (0.4)   DINWOODY FORMATION (NO SIGN)

13.3 (1.0)   PARK CITY FORMATION SIGN

15.1 (1.8)   **PHOSPHATE OVERLOOK. STOP:**

Turn into scenic turnoff on the west side of the highway. This kiosk contains information regarding the phosphate mining operations. In addition, you can see much of the geology that you have driven through to the south. Most notable are the rock formations called the "Red Fleet." These are three features formed in the upper Chinle Formation and Nugget Sandstone that have the appearance of battleships plying their way through the sea. The bows and decks are the upper unnamed member of the Chinle, and the turrets are the Nugget Sandstone.

WILDLIFE VIEWING #2

Elevation: 6,490 feet

Both this and the next stop, Windy Point, are good areas for viewing elk and deer, especially during the winter and spring (December to June).

PLANTS:

As the Byway begins to climb the slopes, the desert shrub community intergrades with pinyon-juniper, almost exclusively juniper in this area. Cold air pools in the Uinta Basin during winter inversions, restricting the growth of frost-sensitive pinyon pine.

After stop, return to U.S. 191 and continue north up the hill.

17.4 (2.3)   **WINDY POINT OVERLOOK. STOP:**

Geologic and ecologic turnout and kiosk on south side of highway. The surrounding rocks are still in the Park City Formation.

WILDLIFE VIEWING #3

Elevation: 7,171 feet

See wildlife information at previous stop.

After stop, continue north up the hill.

18.9 (1.5)   **WEBER SANDSTONE SIGN**

19.2 (0.3)   **STOP:**

Use the turnout on the north side of the highway to view the Gilbert Peak erosion surface and Tertiary (Oligocene) Bishop Conglomerate. The Gilbert Peak erosion surface is the sharp unconformity (erosion surface with missing rock record) between the Pennsylvanian–Permian Weber Sandstone and the Oligocene Bishop Conglomerate.

PLANTS:

The mountain shrub community is predominant here.

After stop, continue up the hill.

20.4 (1.2) **RED CLOUD PULLOUT. STOP:**

Junction with the Red Cloud Loop and East Park Reservoir roads on the west side of the highway. Here the Scenic Byway is on the Diamond Mountain Plateau sector of the Uinta Mountains. Note the relatively flat surface that includes large boulders scattered about the landscape. These boulders are part of the Pleistocene gravel deposit. Erosion by the imperceptible winnowing of the fine-grained material in the deposit by rain and snowmelt waters reduces the thickness of the deposit over time; however, the boulders are too big to be carried off by this erosion process and are left behind as lag material. You may notice that the Diamond Mountain Plateau looks fairly flat from a distance, but up close it is quite undulating due to erosion that has dissected the plateau surface.

WILDLIFE VIEWING #4

Elevation: 8,089 feet

Watch for deer, elk, grouse, eagles, songbirds, and small mammals.

PLANTS:

Sagebrush is the prevalent shrub here, and a few aspen clones are beginning to appear; the meadows are a good site for spring wildflowers.

After stop, return to U.S. 191 and continue north.

Blue Grouse
Ron Stewart

22.4 (2.0) **ROAD CUT IN THE ROUND VALLEY LIMESTONE**

22.5 (0.1) The large pile of limestone boulders on the west side of the road is being used as ballast on the toe of a landslide to prevent the slide from moving onto the road. The landslide is in the Mississippian Doughnut Shale, which is a clay-rich mudstone and shale formation.

22.6 (0.1) **LITTLE BRUSH CREEK TRAILHEAD**
Little Brush Creek trailhead in the Doughnut Shale. The highway crosses the bed of Little Brush Creek, which is usually dry here because the creek plunges into a sinkhole in the Madison Limestone. Sinkholes and caves are common in the Madison Limestone in the Uinta Mountains. They are examples of karst topography caused by dissolution of the limestone by groundwater. You can see down to Little Brush Creek Cave by walking about a quarter-mile up the trail (watch for off-road vehicles). **Caving is a dangerous activity and should only be attempted by those parties who are experienced and well equipped.**
Stay on U.S. 191, unless you stop to walk.

22.8 (0.2) **ROAD CUT IN MISSISSIPPIAN HUMBUG FORMATION**

24.8 (2.0) Junction of Diamond Mountain road
Stay on U.S. 191.

24.9 (0.1) **MADISON FORMATION SIGN ON WEST (MADISON LIMESTONE)**
Outcrops of the Madison Limestone are up the hill beyond the retaining wall.

25.0 (0.1) **ASPEN NATURE TRAIL. STOP:**

B The turnout on the east has a short, fairly level nature trail that interprets the diverse and colorful life found among the aspens.
WILDLIFE VIEWING #5
Elevation: 8,239 feet
Spring fawning area—watch for deer with fawns, especially around dawn and dusk. This is also an important birding site, especially for tree swallows.
PLANTS:
Good example of an aspen forest, with an understory of sagebrush,

snowberry, and dwarf juniper. Look for wildflowers such as lupine, blue columbine, yarrow, and wild geranium in the spring and summer.

After stop, return to U.S. 191 and continue north.

Ron Stewart

25.5 (0.5) **LODORE FORMATION SIGN**
The Lodore is poorly exposed through this area.

26.2 (0.7) **SUMMIT AND UINTAH–DAGGETT COUNTY LINE**

Highest point on the Scenic Byway, elevation 8,428 feet. This marks the Uintah–Daggett County line and the modern summit and drainage divide. The crest of the eastern Uinta Mountains and drainage divide have not always been at this location. They have changed positions the past 30 million years as uplift ended and tectonic extension began. The drainage system adjusted to the changing landscape as the ancestral crest of the range moved downward on a fault block. The broad valley east of the highway is a part of a relic drainage system that flowed southward about 30 million years ago. Now, the streams within the broad valley, and north of the modern divide, flow northward. The rocks in the hills surrounding this section of highway are the Neoproterozoic Uinta Mountain Group.

PLANTS:
Lodgepole pine is the dominant conifer along here, often in dense "dog-hair" stands of uniform age. Aspens are interspersed here and there.

29.1 (2.9) **CART CREEK PULLOUT. STOP:**

 The turnout on the west side of the highway has interpretive exhibits on ecology.

 WILDLIFE VIEWING #6
Elevation: 8,090 feet

 Large herds of deer and elk may be seen in the spring and fall. This is also used as a fawning and calving area.

PLANTS:
The meadow features silver sage, *Artemisia cana*, which has long pointed leaves, unlike the three-toothed leaves of the taller, more common big sagebrush, *Artemisia tridentata*. Extensive lodgepole forests cover the slopes above.
After stop, continue north on U.S. 191.

32.0 (2.9) **UINTA MOUNTAIN GROUP SIGN**

35.5 (3.5) Greendale Junction
The intersection of U.S. 191 and State Road 44. Turn north (right) to continue on U.S. Highway 191 and travel to Flaming Gorge Dam, Dutch John, and Minnies Gap.
The rest of this section of the road guide follows U.S. 191 to the Utah–Wyoming state line. If you are traveling west to Manila, Utah, reset your odometer to zero at this junction, then turn to the S.R. 44-43 segment of the road guide (page 143).

35.6 (0.1) **GREENDALE JUNCTION PORTAL. STOP:**

B Pullout on the east side of the highway with Scenic Byway information and exhibits describing regional geology and wildlife.

Deer, elk, and marmots are frequently seen along, and sometimes on, this stretch of road; watch carefully for them, especially in early morning and evening hours.

PLANTS:

Note how the forest becomes more open, with majestic, widely spaced trees and an understory of grasses and small shrubs—a classic ponderosa pine community.

After stop, continue north on U.S. 191.

36.2 (0.6) **SWETT RANCH ROAD**

Side road to the Swett Ranch historic site; check with Ashley National Forest for hours of operation.

Stay on U.S. 191, unless visiting the ranch.

The Swett Ranch historic site preserves old cabins, barns, and farm implements.
Ron Stewart/Courtesy UDWR

36.3 (0.1)   OUTCROPS OF SHALE AND SANDSTONE BEDS
OF UINTA MOUNTAIN GROUP

38.3 (2.0)   FIREFIGHTERS MEMORIAL PULLOUT. STOP:

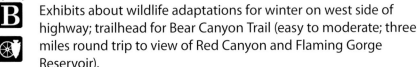

Exhibits about wildlife adaptations for winter on west side of highway; trailhead for Bear Canyon Trail (easy to moderate; three miles round trip to view of Red Canyon and Flaming Gorge Reservoir).

HISTORY:

Firefighters Memorial Campground on east side of highway. On Loop C (to the right) is a memorial plaque honoring three men who died while fighting the Cart Creek Fire in 1977. (No campground fee required if you are just visiting the memorial.)

After stop, continue north on U.S. 191.

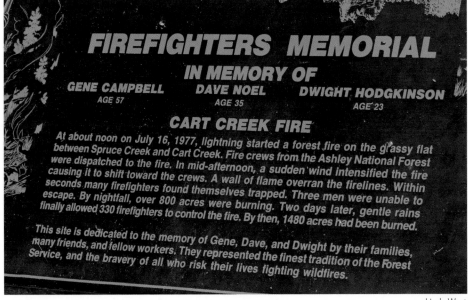

FIREFIGHTERS MEMORIAL

IN MEMORY OF

GENE CAMPBELL   DAVE NOEL   DWIGHT HODGKINSON
AGE 57   AGE 35   AGE 23

CART CREEK FIRE

At about noon on July 16, 1977, lightning started a forest fire on the grassy flat between Spruce Creek and Cart Creek. Fire crews from the Ashley National Forest were dispatched to the fire. In mid-afternoon, a sudden wind intensified the fire causing it to shift toward the crews. A wall of flame overran the firelines. Within seconds many firefighters found themselves trapped. Three men were unable to escape. By nightfall, over 800 acres were burning. Two days later, gentle rains finally allowed 330 firefighters to control the fire. By then, 1480 acres had been burned.

This site is dedicated to the memory of Gene, Dave, and Dwight by their families, many friends, and fellow workers. They represented the finest tradition of the Forest Service, and the bravery of all who risk their lives fighting wildfires.

Linda West

39.2 (0.9)   CEDAR SPRINGS OVERLOOK. STOP:

Use the pullout on the north side of the highway to view the Uinta Mountain Group and Uinta fault across Flaming Gorge Reservoir. The Uinta Mountain Group forms the outcrops seen from here northward across the reservoir. The lighter-colored mountain in the distance to the north is composed of Triassic–Jurassic Nugget Sandstone. The Uinta fault runs along the base of the mountain and separates the Nugget Sandstone from the Uinta Mountain Group.

PLANTS:

As the road descends, the plant communities gradually change from ponderosa pine to pinyon-juniper. Pinyon pines are more common here than on the south slope, because severe winter inversions occur less often here than in the cold-air "sink" of the Uinta Basin.

After stop, continue north on U.S. 191.

The Uinta Mountains largely formed by upward movement along the Uinta and other fault zones during a mountain-building event called the Laramide orogeny. The Neoproterozoic Uinta Mountain Group moved upward and was placed next to the Triassic–Jurassic Nugget Sandstone along this segment of the Uinta fault. The Laramide orogeny in this region spanned about 30 million years (Late Cretaceous to Oligocene). View north from Cedar Springs Overlook.

Doug Sprinkel

40.4 (1.2) **BROWNS PARK SIGN REFERRING TO THE ROAD CUT**
The Browns Park Formation is middle Miocene (about 10 to 12 million years old).

41.1 (0.7) **CART CREEK BRIDGE OVER FLAMING GORGE RESERVOIR**
Look for ospreys, which have sometimes nested on the bridge.

41.7 (0.6) **FLAMING GORGE DAM VISITOR CENTER. STOP:**
The Visitor Center contains displays and publications about Flaming Gorge Dam and Reservoir and other regional information. Ask Visitor Center personnel for times of dam tours. Contact the U.S. Bureau of Reclamation for more information about Visitor Center hours and dam operations.
WILDLIFE VIEWING #7A
At the reservoir, look for various water-dependent bird species, such as osprey, ducks, Canada geese, and during the winter months, bald eagles.
After stop, return to U.S. 191 and continue to Dutch John, Utah.

42.1 (0.4) **TURN RIGHT ON RIVER ACCESS ROAD FOR DAM VIEWPOINT**
WILDLIFE VIEWING #7B
Elevation: 6,071 feet
Taking a walk down the Little Hole Trail (reached from lower down the road, after the viewpoint) along the Green River greatly increases the chances for viewing river otters and the fish they prey upon. The stretch of river below the dam is also a Blue Ribbon trout fishery and is very popular with anglers as well as boaters.

42.8 (0.7) The road cut on the west side of the highway exposes a fault in the Uinta Mountain Group.

43.4 (0.6) The burnt trees in this area are from the 2002 Mustang Ridge fire. The fire was started along the highway near Mustang Ridge when a motorist lost a wheel off his trailer, and sparks ignited the dry grass beside the road. With extremely dry fuel due to several years of drought, the fire quickly spread and ultimately burned 20,038 acres.

River otter
Ron Stewart

What Did the Fish Say When It Hit the Concrete Wall?

Flaming Gorge Dam was constructed from 1958 to 1964 on the Green River. The dam is about forty-two miles from Vernal, Utah, and about six miles south of the Utah–Wyoming state line. It is a medium-thick-arch concrete dam that has a structural height of 502 feet and a crest length of 1,180 feet. The crest width is twenty-seven feet and the base widens to 131 feet according to U.S. Bureau of Reclamation. The volume of concrete used to construct the dam was 986,600 cubic yards.

Impoundment of the Green River created Flaming Gorge Reservoir, which stretches ninety-one miles from the dam to near Green River, Wyoming. The capacity of the reservoir is 3,788,900 acre-feet at a maintained surface elevation of 6,040 feet. The water is more than 400 feet deep at the dam, about 300 feet deep near the Red Canyon Overlook, and about 180 feet deep in the middle of the reservoir east of Linwood Bay. The primary purpose of the reservoir is to generate electricity, store irrigation water, and provide recreation.

Flaming Gorge Dam was constructed in the Uinta Mountain Group. The rocks at the dam site dip about 16 degrees north and consist of red quartzite, sandstone, and thin to thick interbedded shale. Because of the interbedded shale in the abutments, special foundation treatment was performed to stabilize the shale zones. Two fault zones are in the dam site area, but neither cuts through the abutments. One of the faults, however, is about eighty-two feet upstream from the dam.

Flaming Gorge Dam impounds the Green River. The dam abutments are in the reddish sandstone beds of the Neoproterozoic Uinta Mountain Group. View north from dam overlook off U.S. 191.
Doug Sprinkel

44.3 (0.9) **DUTCH JOHN**

The town was built in 1957 for the construction workers who built Flaming Gorge Dam. Dutch John was named for "Dutch John" Honselena (who was really *Deutsch*, or German), a horse trader who grazed his stock all along the slopes above Flaming Gorge around the 1860s.
Stay on U.S. 191.

45.3 (1.0) The road cut on the north side of the highway exposes beds of the Uinta Mountain Group. Note the interbedded green shales. This is one of the sites where the shale beds produced microscopic fossils of several species of primitive cyanobacteria (Utah's oldest known fossils).

48.3 (3.0) **STOP:**

Use the pullout on the south side of the road to view the Uinta fault zone. The Uinta Mountain Group is exposed and deformed along the east end of the road cut. Westward, the Uinta fault has formed a zone of fault gouge—pulverized rock resulting from movement along the fault. The west end of the road cut includes deformed beds of the Triassic Chinle Formation. The Nugget Sandstone forms the cliffs above the road cut.
Continue north on U.S. 191.

48.4 (0.1) The Scenic Byway cuts through vertical beds of the Triassic–Jurassic Nugget Sandstone. These beds are vertical because the upward movement of the Uinta Mountains along the Uinta fault had enough force to push the Nugget Sandstone to its present position.

48.5 (0.1) **NUGGET SANDSTONE (NAVAJO FORMATION)**

48.6 (0.1) **DAKOTA SANDSTONE (DAKOTA FORMATION sign)**

49.0 (0.4) Road cut through the Cretaceous Frontier Sandstone. The drainage on the east side of the highway just before the road cut contains the underlying Mowry Shale.

49.3 (0.3) **ANTELOPE FLAT OVERLOOK. STOP:**

B

Ⅱ

Pullout for interpretive exhibits and views of Antelope Flat and Flaming Gorge. The Cretaceous Baxter Shale (Mancos Shale equivalent) comprises Antelope Flat; however, modern wind-blown sand and alluvium cover the Baxter Shale in many places.

WILDLIFE VIEWING #8

Elevation: 6,476 feet

Deer, elk, pronghorn, and jackrabbits use this area, especially during the spring and winter months.

PLANTS:

Desert shrub community, with sagebrush predominant.

Continue north on U.S. 191.

49.9 (0.6) **BAXTER SHALE (HILLIARD–MANCOS FORMATION SIGN)**

This is the Baxter Shale; the Hilliard Shale is restricted to the Evanston area in the western Green River Basin of Wyoming, and the Mancos is restricted to south of the Uinta Mountains.

52.5 (2.6) **UTAH–WYOMING STATE LINE**

The base of the Cretaceous Mesaverde Group is exposed. The Mesaverde Group forms the hill ahead called The Glades; locally, it is called the Devil's Racetrack. The Mesaverde Group includes the basal Blair Sandstone overlain by the Rock Springs Formation, which is overlain by the Ericson Sandstone.

53.1 (0.6) Intersection of the Clay Basin road on the east side of the highway, and the top of the Mesaverde Group. The road cut that U.S. Highway 191 goes through is called Minnies Gap.

END U.S. HIGHWAY 191 SEGMENT

UTAH STATE ROADS 44–43 SEGMENT

Road guide for the Flaming Gorge-Uintas National Scenic Byway, State Roads 44 and 43 from Greendale Junction to Manila, Utah, and on to Lucerne Marina. The trip is about fifty miles long and should take about two hours depending on the number of stops. A more detailed geologic guide to this segment can be found in Utah Geological Association Publication 33 (see the reference list).

At Greendale Junction, reset your trip odometer to zero and travel west on S.R. 44.

Cumulative Miles
(Incremental Miles)
Icon(s)

Description

0.0 (0.0)   **GREENDALE JUNCTION**

Intersection of U.S. Highway 191 and Utah S.R. 44. The rocks surrounding the area are red sandstone beds of the middle Neoproterozoic Uinta Mountain Group.
WILDLIFE VIEWING #9
Elevation: 7,490 feet (at junction)
The section of Utah S.R. 44 from Greendale Junction to Moose Ponds (mile 14.5) is a high-use area for deer, elk, and especially moose. Wild turkeys may also be seen along this stretch.
Use caution, especially when traveling at night, as the animals frequently cross the highway!

Wild turkeys can sometimes be seen along S.R. 44 from Greendale Junction to Sheep Creek.
Linda West

0.9 (0.9)   **GREENDALE OVERLOOK. STOP:**

Scenic Byway exhibits on the north side of the highway describe how fire and water shape landscape and life here. Parts of several historic ranches are visible, including Swett Ranch at the far right.

3.4 (2.5)   **RED CANYON ROAD**

Turn right (north) on Forest Service road 95 to the Red Canyon Overlook and Visitor Center.

Red Canyon Lodge is also located down this road. You will note that the road is built on a relatively flat surface. This is the Gilbert Peak erosion surface. More will be discussed at the Red Canyon Overlook stop.

PLANTS:

Widely spaced ponderosa pines, with occasional aspen clones, predominate along this side road and the adjacent stretch of Highway 44.

4.7 (1.3)   **WEST GREENS LAKE NATURE TRAIL. STOP:**

Exhibits along this short, easy trail feature the lake and the value of wetlands for wildlife.

6.0 (1.3)   **RED CANYON VISITOR CENTER AND OVERLOOK. STOP:**

Displays, publications, general information, and restrooms are available at the Visitor Center; contact Ashley National Forest for Visitor Center seasons and hours. Walk to the end of the asphalt path for a view down into Red Canyon and Flaming Gorge Reservoir. Across the canyon to the north is Bare Top Mountain (shown on topographic maps as Bear Mountain; after a fire burned off most of the trees on top of it, locals began calling it Bare Top. The U.S. Board on Geographic Names formally recognized the name Bare Top Mountain in 1988).

You will notice a relatively flat surface on Bare Top Mountain; this surface is the same surface that you drove across to get to the overlook. The surface continues west at about at the same elevation as where you are standing. This is the Gilbert Peak erosion surface, which formed about 30 million years ago when uplift of the Uinta Mountains concluded. The Gilbert Peak erosion surface on Bare Top Mountain is about 7,730 feet in elevation, but remnants of this surface in Wyoming, about ten to fifteen miles north, are between about 8,600 and 9,100 feet in elevation. The Gilbert Peak erosion surface should be higher here than its remnants in Wyoming because the surface should slope northward away from the Uintas. So, why is the Gilbert Peak erosion surface lower in elevation here? The answer is that the eastern Uinta Mountains have likely been lowered relative to the area to the north, principally along the Uinta fault zone. By about middle Miocene time (about 15 to 10 million years ago), the Gilbert Peak erosion surface was lowered a minimum of 870 to 1,370 feet and possibly as much as 3,200 feet (see Hansen, 1986, for details). This apparent lowering of the eastern Uinta Mountains also played an important role in the change of the regional drainage pattern and capture of the Green River.

Red Canyon, which was named by Major John Wesley Powell on his historic trip down the Green and Colorado Rivers in 1869, is about 1,700 feet deep. The bottom of what used to be the Green River would be about another 300 feet lower. The story of how and when Red Canyon formed is fascinating. First, the Green River is one of only a few rivers that actually flow *toward* a major mountain range. This has been the source of geologic discussions since Major Powell first noticed this unusual fact. Wally Hansen, a prominent geologist with the U.S. Geological Survey, described what many geologists generally believe happened (see Hansen, 1986, for details).

Hansen suggested that the Green River originally did not flow through Red Canyon; instead, it flowed out of the Wind River Mountains to Green River, Wyoming (as it does today), but then turned eastward through southern Wyoming. Some geologists

(The following pages) The view from Red Canyon overlook shows the relatively flat Gilbert Peak erosion surface at the base of the higher Uinta peaks. Streams originally flowed northward, away from the peaks, but as mountain uplift ended and the eastern Uintas subsided, a small stream began flowing eastward across the Gilbert Peak surface. After capturing the ancestral upper Green River, the enlarged stream could erode more vigorously, and began cutting Red Canyon. Ron Stewart

speculate that this ancestral Green River flowed to the North Platte River and was part of the Mississippi River drainage system prior to Miocene time. Lowering of the Uinta Mountains as described above formed a new east-west drainage (Red Canyon creek) that flowed eastward to Browns Park and divided the north-flowing streams that drained off the Uinta highlands to the Green River Basin of Wyoming; streams north of Red Canyon creek reversed their flow southward into the newly formed Red Canyon. Red Canyon creek incised its way northward by headward erosion, and perhaps by less than 2 million years ago captured the Green River. Now the Green River flowed through Red Canyon and into Browns Park, but it still was not connected to the Colorado River system. The Green River finally became part of the Colorado River system probably less than 1 million years ago (by about early Pleistocene) when it was diverted into Lodore Canyon.

The large vertical cracks or joints that run through the red sandstone along the edge of the canyon are expansion joints. They form from small cracks and are enlarged by freeze-thaw processes and gravity. Eventually, the rocks on the canyon side of the joint will collapse into the canyon. This is an example of mechanical weathering and is the principal process that widens Red Canyon.

WILDLIFE VIEWING #10
Elevation: 7,416 feet
The use of a spotting scope or binoculars may help you sight elk grazing on Bare Top Mountain, directly across the gorge. Also watch for turkey vultures, osprey, falcons, blue grouse, and bighorn sheep. On a smaller scale, marmots, chipmunks, hummingbirds, and lizards may be seen.
Return to S.R. 44.

8.6 (2.6)   Intersection with S.R. 44
Turn right (west) onto S.R. 44 and continue toward Manila, Utah.

14.5 (5.9) **Moose Ponds Pullout. STOP:**

B Turnout on south side of highway for exhibits about wildlife.
Wildlife viewing #11

🔭 Elevation: 8,077 feet
Watch for osprey, belted kingfishers, and ducks, which utilize the ponds in this area.

🍃 **Plants:**
Ponderosa pines give way to slender, densely spaced lodgepole pines along this stretch.
Continue west on S.R. 44.

17.4 (2.9) One of several faults that cut the Uinta Mountain Group is in the road cut on the west side of the highway.

17.6 (0.2) **Stop:**
Use the pullout on the north side of the highway to view an anticline in the Uinta Mountain Group. The arched-up rocks in the Uinta Mountain Group form a fold called an anticline. It formed here because nearby faulting created enough compressive stresses in the rocks to bend the beds upward.
Continue on S.R. 44.

A small anticline (arch-shaped fold) formed in the Neoproterozoic Uinta Mountain Group. Movement on several nearby faults and associated tectonic forces squeezed the rocks in this area to form the anticline. View southwest near Carter Creek on S.R. 44.

Doug Sprinkel

18.2 (0.6)   UINTA MOUNTAIN GROUP SIGN

18.8 (0.6)   DOWD MOUNTAIN

Intersection of the Dowd Mountain road (Forest Service road 94), which travels across another section of the Gilbert Peak erosion surface cut on the red sandstone beds of the Uinta Mountain Group. The road (graded dirt; use caution when wet) leads about four miles to an overlook with superb views of Flaming Gorge Reservoir and the surrounding country.

WILDLIFE VIEWING #12

Elevation: 7,552 feet

Deer, elk, and moose may be sighted along the route to the overlook, which provides a good view of Bare Top Mountain with the potential for elk and deer viewing. Small mammals, blue grouse and other birds, and bighorn sheep may also be seen in the area.

PLANTS:

The road to the viewpoint also passes through diverse plant communities: ponderosa pine, Douglas-fir, pinyon-juniper, and mountain shrub, the last including sagebrush, bitterbrush, and mountain mahogany.

Stay on S.R. 44, unless you take the side trip to the overlook.

The Dowd Mountain overlook offers fine views of the Flaming Gorge country.
Linda West

The Neoproterozoic Uinta Mountain Group moved upward and was placed next to the Mississippian Madison Limestone and Doughnut-Humbug Formations along this segment of the Uinta fault. View west from a turnout along S.R. 44 along Spring Creek.

Doug Sprinkel

19.2 (0.4) Traveling north, the dips in the Uinta Mountain Group are increasing or getting steeper northward. What lies ahead?

19.6 (0.4) **DOWDS HOLE PULLOUT. STOP:**

Turn west onto Forest Service road 218 for exhibits on geology and wildlife. This road is the east end of the Sheep Creek Geologic Loop, which continues west and north for 12.5 miles and rejoins S.R. 44 near Manila.

PLANTS:
Mountain shrubs (sagebrush and rabbitbrush) mixed with grasses dominate the meadows here, with junipers and ponderosas dotting the slopes a little higher up.

To keep following this road log, return now to S.R. 44 and continue toward Manila.

20.4 (0.8) **STOP:**
The brake-check area on the north side of the highway offers a great view of the Uinta fault zone. The Uinta fault pushed the Uinta Mountain Group next to the Mississippian Humbug and Doughnut Formations. The fault trace goes down the valley north of the pullout.

Continue on S.R. 44.

20.9 (0.5) **STOP:**
The pullout on the east side of the highway offers a close view of the Uinta fault zone and deformed bedding in Uinta Mountain Group (on south) and Doughnut Shale (on north). The Uinta fault is a zone in which the Uinta Mountain Group has been pulverized as the rocks moved up along the fault. The dark-gray shale beds of the Mississippian Doughnut Shale, as well as the overlying Pennsylvanian Round Valley Limestone, are all dipping steeply to the north or are vertical.
Continue north on S.R. 44 to Manila, Utah.

21.1 (0.2) Vertical beds of the Round Valley Limestone are exposed on the north side of the highway.

21.2 (0.1) The Weber Sandstone is the light-colored sandstone exposed along the highway and in road cuts.

22.6 (1.4) **SHEEP CREEK OVERLOOK. STOP:**

Turn west into the overlook, which offers great views of Flaming Gorge Reservoir and lower Sheep Creek Canyon, and includes exhibits on the geologic formations and the prehistoric life found in them. Watch for bighorn sheep, which are often seen from here on down to Sheep Creek.
Continue north on S.R. 44 to Manila, Utah.

24.6 (2.0) **PARK CITY FORMATION SIGN**

25.1 (0.5) **DINWOODY FORMATION**
This forms the gray shale slopes along the highway.

26.1 (1.0) **THE MOENKOPI FORMATION**
This formation is well exposed on the south side of the highway. The beds, mostly fine-grained sandstone, are steeply tilted and offer a view of the bed top. The pattern surface on the bed top is a good example of ripple marks. Ripple marks are formed by running water in streams or by wave action along a shoreline. Close examination of the ripple marks reveals they are tilted slightly in one direction or are asymmetrical, a shape commonly made by

(Above) Sheep Creek flows eastward (toward the lower right corner of photograph) across the relatively soft Moenkopi and Chinle Formations, forming a classic strike valley. Left (south) of Sheep Creek is a monocline formed in the Park City Formation. A monocline is a fold where the otherwise shallow dips of beds locally become steeper. Monoclines in this area are usually formed by movement of subsurface faults. View west from S.R. 44. Doug Sprinkel

(Below) Permian Park City Formation through the Triassic–Jurassic Nugget Sandstone surround Flaming Gorge Reservoir. During his historic boat trip down the Green and Colorado rivers in 1869, Major John Wesley Powell named Flaming Gorge for the brilliant red Triassic rocks exposed at the mouth of the gorge. View north from S.R. 44. Doug Sprinkel

The patterned surface on the bed top of the Triassic Moenkopi Formation is a good example of ripple marks. Ripple marks are formed by water movement in stream or shallow-marine environments. Close examination of these ripple marks reveals they are current ripples, made by water currents flowing in one direction instead of wave ripples made by water sloshing back and forth. View south near Manns Campground along S.R. 44. Doug Sprinkel

streams flowing in one direction; symmetrical ripple marks are formed by water sloshing back and forth and are commonly made by waves.

26.7 (0.6) **SHEEP CREEK CANYON NATURE TRAIL. STOP:**

  Just across the bridge is a parking area with restrooms. A short nature trail leads across Sheep Creek on a foot bridge; trailside exhibits explain the value of riparian (stream-side) areas to both wildlife and humans.

WILDLIFE VIEWING #13
Elevation: 6,239 feet
From late August through September, the Kokanee salmon may be seen swimming up Sheep Creek for their annual spawn. Also keep an eye out for bighorn sheep, wild turkeys, songbirds, and a variety of reptiles.

Bighorn ewe and lamb
Ron Stewart

26.8 (0.1) Almost opposite the parking area is the turnoff to the west for the Sheep Creek Geologic Loop, a fascinating drive that follows Sheep Creek up a narrow canyon, then climbs to the higher forests and meadows and returns to S.R. 44 at the Dowds Hole Pullout. Even if you choose not to drive the full loop, we recommend a short side trip as far as the following three points.

Note: The Sheep Creek Geologic Loop is closed from approximately December 20–April 20, dependent on snow conditions. Early spring and late fall visitors should check with Ashley National Forest for road conditions or closures.

29.0 (2.2) **DOWD'S GRAVE**
Homesteader Cleophas J. Dowd and two of his children are buried here.

31.8 (2.8) **BIG SPRING**
 WILDLIFE VIEWING #14
Elevation: 6,897 feet
Sheep Creek is an excellent area for viewing Rocky Mountain

bighorn sheep. Look in open grassy areas along the stream and the base of cliffs. The bat cave (see "Bats" under "Wildlife Fun Facts," page 76) above Big Spring provides the opportunity of viewing bats at dusk from April through September. The stream and subsequent large trees also make this an excellent birding area.

32.2 (0.4)   PALISADES MEMORIAL PARK

This site was a campground until the night of June 9, 1965. Heavy rains combined with an unusually deep and still-melting snowpack caused a debris flow—a slurry of rocks, mud, and water—that swept down the canyon, killing the family that was camped here and leaving jumbled piles of boulders and silt along the creek. Following this tragedy, the Forest Service designated the site as day-use only to reduce the risk to visitors in case of future debris flows.

Return to S.R. 44.

Fluctuating, shallow Jurassic seas dominated the region and flooded the extensive sand dune deposits of the Nugget Sandstone. The Carmel Formation records the first incursion and retreat; the lower part is limestone with many marine invertebrate fossils, and the upper part is mudstone, siltstone, and abundant gypsum indicating a tidal flat. The Entrada Sandstone records the return of coastal sand dunes, which were subsequently flooded by the Stump sea. View north at Sheep Creek Gap on S.R. 44.
Doug Sprinkel

37.6 (5.4) Junction with S.R. 44
Turn left (north) and continue to Manila, Utah.

37.7 (0.1) SHEEP CREEK GAP
The highway cuts through Sheep Creek Gap, its "gates" formed of Nugget Sandstone ("Navajo" on the sign just north of the gap).

38.0 (0.3) CARMEL FORMATION SIGN

38.8 (0.8) ENTRADA SANDSTONE SIGN
The Flaming Gorge National Recreation Area boundary is just north of it.

40.0 (1.2) STUMP FORMATION (CURTIS FORMATION SIGN)
Forty years ago, geologists thought this was the Curtis Formation, but additional research since then has demonstrated that only the lower sandstone is the Curtis Member, while the upper greenish shale and capping limestone are the Redwater Member of the Stump Formation. The sign is on the Redwater Member.

40.6 (0.6) MORRISON FORMATION SIGN
The sign and outcrops on both sides of the highway.

41.0 (0.4) DAKOTA SANDSTONE SIGN
The sign and outcrops in the road cut.

41.3 (0.3) FRONTIER SANDSTONE SIGN

42.7 (1.4) BAXTER SHALE (MANCOS SHALE SIGN)
This sign is incorrect because geologists have determined this to be the Baxter Shale; the Mancos is restricted to south of the Uinta Mountains.

43.3 (0.6) MANILA
Manila is the county seat of Daggett County and serves as the gateway to Flaming Gorge Reservoir. The reddish-colored hills north of Manila are composed of the Tertiary Wasatch Formation.

The town is built on the alluvium-covered Baxter Shale. The Henrys Fork fault is near the base of the hills and pushed the Baxter Shale up against the Wasatch Formation.

43.4 (0.1)   S.R. 44–43 JUNCTION
The Forest Service Flaming Gorge Ranger District Office on the southwest (left) corner has area information.
Turn right (east) on S.R. 43. Drive across alluvium-covered Baxter Shale.

46.5 (3.1)   HENRYS FORK RIVER

HISTORY:
The river was named for Major Andrew Henry, business partner of William H. Ashley. In 1825, after floating the Green River from this area to the Uinta Basin, Ashley organized the first trappers' rendezvous, which met on the Henrys Fork several miles west of here.
WILDLIFE VIEWING #15
Elevation: 6,110 feet
Large concentrations of bald eagles may be observed during the winter months.

47.1 (0.6)   INTERSECTION OF S.R. 43 AND LUCERNE VALLEY ROAD.
Turn right (east) onto Lucerne Valley Road.
The road cut on the west exposes the Cretaceous Rock Springs Formation of the Mesaverde Group.

47.5 (0.4)   ERICSON SANDSTONE OF MESAVERDE GROUP

47.6 (0.1)   Wasatch Formation is north of the road and Ericson Sandstone is south of the road.

48.4 (0.8) LINWOOD OVERLOOK. STOP:

 Use the pullout to view Linwood Bay and the Nugget Sandstone through Morrison Formation exposed across the bay.

 HISTORY:
When Flaming Gorge Reservoir filled, the rising waters submerged one of Daggett County's two original towns. Linwood, established in 1900 beside the Green River, straddled the Utah–Wyoming line. So did its schoolhouse, giving it the distinction of being the only known school run by the school boards of two different states. The school building was moved before the town was flooded.

PLANTS:
Desert shrub community predominates on the flats between the overlook and reservoir.

Continue east on Lucerne Valley road.

Tilted and slightly folded strata of the Cretaceous Mesaverde Group form The Glades, also locally known as the Devil's Racetrack. The Mesaverde Group comprises (from top down) the Ericson Sandstone, Rock Springs Formation, and Blair Sandstone. The Mesaverde Group rests on the Cretaceous Baxter Shale as seen on Antelope Flat. View is east from the Lucerne peninsula between the Linwood turnout and Lucerne Marina.
Doug Sprinkel

50.9 (2.5) LUCERNE PENINSULA AND MARINA
WILDLIFE VIEWING #16
Elevation: 6,174 feet
The Lucerne Peninsula provides good viewing of bald eagles
during the winter months (November to January), and pronghorn,
white-tailed jackrabbits, and small mammals throughout the year.

END UTAH STATE ROADS 44–43 SEGMENT

Pronghorn doe and triplets
Ron Stewart/Courtesy UDWR

Linda West

BIBLIOGRAPHY

GEOLOGY

The geologic history in this guide was summarized from the work of numerous geologists who have studied and mapped the rocks in the region. Below are the key references that were used. These publications provide more detailed information about the geology of this fascinating area.

Boardman, R. S., and Cheetham, A. H., 1987, "Phylum Bryozoa," in Boardman, R. S., Cheetham, A. H., and Rowell, A. J., eds., *Fossil Invertebrates*: Palo Alto, California, Blackwell Scientific Publications, p. 497–549.

Bradley, W. H., 1936, "Geomorphology of the North Flank of the Uinta Mountains": U.S. Geological Survey Professional Paper 185-I, p. 163–199.

———, 1964, "Geology of the Green River Formation and Associated Eocene Rocks in Southwestern Wyoming and Adjacent Parts of Colorado and Utah": U.S. Geological Survey Professional Paper 496-B, 86 p.

Buchsbaum, R., Buchsbaum, M., Pearse, J., and Pearse, V., 1988, *Animals Without Backbones* (3rd ed.): Chicago, University of Chicago Press, 405 p.

DeCourten, F., 1998, *Dinosaurs of Utah*: Salt Lake City, University of Utah Press, 300 p.

Dehler, C. M., Pederson, J. L., Sprinkel, D. A., and Kowallis, B. J., eds., 2005, *Uinta Mountain Geology*: Utah Geological Association Publication 33, 447 p.

Emmons, S. F., 1877, "Descriptive Geology": U.S. Geological Exploration 40th Parallel (King), Vol. 2, p. 890.

Gunnell, G. F., and Bartels, W. S., 1999, "Middle Eocene Vertebrates From the Uinta Basin, Utah, and Their Relationship with Faunas From the Southern Green River Basin, Wyoming," in Gillette, D. D., ed., *Vertebrate Paleontology in Utah*: Utah Geological Survey Miscellaneous Publication 99-1, p. 429–442.

Hamblin, A. H., and Bilbey, S. A., 1999, "A Dinosaur Track Site in the Navajo-Nugget Sandstone, Red Fleet Reservoir, Uintah County, Utah," in Gillette, D. D., ed., *Vertebrate Paleontology in Utah*: Utah Geological Survey Miscellaneous Publication 99-1, p. 51–58.

Hamblin, A. H., Bilbey, S. A., and Hall, J. E., 2000, "Prehistoric Animal Tracks at Red Fleet State Park, Northeastern Utah," in Sprinkel, D. A., Chidsey, T. C., and Anderson, P. B., eds., *Geology of Utah's Parks and Monuments*: Utah Geological Association Publication 28 (1st ed. only), p. 569–578. (free online access to this article at www.utahgeology.org)

Hansen, W. R., 1965, "Geology of the Flaming Gorge Area, Utah–Colorado–Wyoming": U.S. Geological Survey Professional Paper 490, 196 p.

———, 1975, "The Geologic Story of the Uinta Mountains": *U.S. Geological Survey Bulletin 1291*, 144 p.

———, 1986, "Neogene Tectonics and Geomorphology of the Eastern Uinta Mountains in Utah, Colorado, and Wyoming": U.S. Geological Survey Professional Paper 1356, 78 p.

Hintze, L. F., 1988 (revised 1993), *Geologic History of Utah*: Brigham Young University Geology Studies Special Publication 7, 202 p.

Kirkland, J. I., Cifelli, R. L., Britt, B. B., Burge, D. L., DeCourten, F., Eaton, J. G., and Parrish, J. M., 1999, "Distribution of Vertebrate Faunas in the Cedar Mountain Formation, East-Central Utah," in Gillette, D. D., ed., *Vertebrate Paleontology in Utah*: Utah Geological Survey Miscellaneous Publication 99-1, p. 201–218.

Lockley, M. G., and Peterson, J., 2002, *A Guide to the Fossil Footprints of the World*: Baldwin Park, California, Gem Guides Book Company, 128 p.

Mickelson, D. L., Huntoon, J. E., and Kvale, E. P., 2006, "The Diversity and Stratigraphic Distribution of Pre-Dinosaurian Communities from the Triassic Moenkopi Formation, Utah," in Lucas, S. G., Speilmann, J. A., Hester, P. M., Kenworthy, J. P., and Santucci, V. L., eds., *America's Antiquities—100 Years of Managing Fossils on Federal Lands: New Mexico Museum of Natural History and Sciences Bulletin 34*, p. 132–137.

Murdock, J. N., 1969, "Geology of Flaming Gorge Dam and Reservoir," in Lindsay, J. B., ed., *Geologic Guidebook of the Uinta Mountains—Utah's Maverick Range*: Intermountain Association of Geologists and Utah Geological Society 16th Annual Field Conference, p. 23–31.

Peterson, F., and Turner-Peterson, C. E., 1987, "The Morrison Formation of the Colorado Plateau—Recent Advances in Sedimentology, Stratigraphy, and Paleotectonics": *Hunteria*, Vol. 2, No. 1, p. 1–18.

Pipiringos, G. N., and O'Sullivan, R. B., 1978, "Principal Unconformities in Triassic and Jurassic Rocks, Western Interior United States—a Preliminary Survey": U.S. Geological Survey Professional Paper 1035-A, 29 p.

Pojeta, J., Jr., Runnegar, B., Peel, J. S., and Gordon, M., Jr., 1987, "Phylum Mollusca," in Boardman, R. S., Cheetham, A. H., and Powell, A. J., eds., *Fossil Invertebrates*: Palo Alto, California, Blackwell Scientific Publications, p. 270–435.

Powell, J. W., 1875, *Exploration of the Colorado River and its Tributaries*: Washington, D.C., U.S. Government Printing Office, 218 p.

———, 1876, "Report on the Geology of the Eastern Portion of the Uinta Mountains and a Region of Country Adjacent Thereto": U.S. Geological and Geographical Survey of the Territories (Powell), 218 p.

Rowell, A. J., and Grant, R. E., 1987, "Phylum Brachiopoda," in Boardman, R. S., Cheetham, A. H., and Rowell, A. J., eds., *Fossil Invertebrates*: Palo Alto, California, Blackwell Scientific Publications, p. 445–496.

Schultz, R. J., Lockley, M. G., and Hunt, A. P., 1995, "New Tracksites from the Moenkopi Formation (Lower–Middle Triassic), Glen Canyon National Recreation Area," in Santucci, V. L., ed., National Park Service Paleontological Research, Vol. 2, Technical Report NPS/NPRO/NRTR-93/11, p. 101–106.

Scott, R. L., Santucci, V. L., and Connors, T., 2001, "An Inventory of Paleontological Resources From the National Parks and Monuments in Colorado," in Santucci, V. L., and McClelland, L., eds., Proceedings of the 6th Fossil Resource Conference: National Park Service Technical Report NRS/NRGRD/GRDTR-01/01, p. 178–202.

Sprinkel, D. A., 2000, "Geologic Lake Guide Along Flaming Gorge Reservoir, Flaming Gorge National Recreation Area, Utah–Wyoming," in Anderson, P. B., and Sprinkel, D. A., eds., *Geologic Road, Trail, and Lake Guides to Utah's Parks and Monuments*: Utah Geological Association Publication 29, 1 compact disc.

———, 2003, "Geology of Flaming Gorge National Recreation Area, Utah–Wyoming," in Sprinkel, D. A., Chidsey, T. C., Jr., and Anderson, P. B., eds., *Geology of Utah's Parks and Monuments*: Utah Geological Association Publication 28 (2nd ed.), p. 277–299.

———, 2006, "Interim Geologic Map of the Dutch John 30' x 60' Quadrangle, Daggett and Uintah Counties, Utah, Moffat County, Colorado, and Sweetwater County, Wyoming": Utah Geological Survey Open-File Report 491DM, compact disc, 3 plates, scale 1:100,000.

Sprinkel, D. A., Park, B., and Stevens, M., 2003, "Geology of Sheep Creek Canyon Geologic Area," in Sprinkel, D. A., Chidsey, T. C., Jr., and Anderson, P. B., eds., *Geology of Utah's Parks and Monuments*: Utah Geological Association Publication 28 (2nd ed.), p. 517–528.

Sprinkel, D. A., Kowallis, B. J., Pederson, J. L., and Dehler, C. M., 2005, "Road Guide to the Geology of the Uinta Mountains for the 2005 Utah Geological Association Field Conference," in Dehler, C. M., Pederson, J. L., Sprinkel, D. A., and Kowallis, B. J., eds., *Uinta Mountain Geology*: Utah Geological Association Publication 33, p. 397–447. (free online access to this road guide at www.utahgeology.org)

Sprinkel, J., and Kier, P. M., 1987, "Phylum Echinodermata," in Boardman, R. S., Cheetham, A. H., and Rowell, A. J., eds., *Fossil Invertebrates*: Palo Alto, California, Blackwell Scientific Publications, p. 550–611.

Stidham, T. A., and Holroyd, P. A., 2004, *Turtle Graveyard—A New Diverse Bird Fauna From the Early Eocene Wasatch Formation, Wyoming [abs.]*: Geological Society of America Abstracts with Programs, Vol. 36, No. 5, p. 336.

Stone, D. S., 1993, *Tectonic Evolution of the Uinta Mountains—Palinspastic Restoration of a Structural Cross Section Along Longitude 109°15', Utah*: Utah Geological Survey Miscellaneous Publication 93-8, 19 p.

Tidwell, W. D., 1998, *Common Fossil Plants of Western North America* (2nd ed.): Washington, D.C., Smithsonian Institution Press, 299 p.

U.S. Bureau of Reclamation, 2000, Flaming Gorge Dam: U.S. Bureau of Reclamation DataWeb, http://www.usbr.gov/dataweb/dams/ut10121.htm

PLANTS

Ashley National Forest, 1992, "How to Identify Trees on the Ashley National Forest," USDA Forest Service–Intermountain Region.

Goodrich, S., and Neese, E., 1986, *Uinta Basin Flora*, USDA Forest Service–Intermountain Region, in cooperation with USDA Forest Service–Ashley National Forest and USDI Bureau of Land Management–Vernal District

Taylor, R. J., 1992, *Sagebrush Country: A Wildflower Sanctuary*: Mountain Press Publishing Company.

Robertson, L., 1999, *Southern Rocky Mountain Wildflowers*: Globe Pequot Press.

WILDLIFE

Byers, J. A., 1997, *American Pronghorn Social Adaptations and the Ghosts of Predators Past*: University of Chicago Press.

Canada's Aquatic Environments website: www.aquatic.uoguelph.ca, CyberNatural Software Group, University of Guelph.

Channel Islands National Park website: www.nps.gov/chis/naturescience/townsends-bats.htm

Chapman, J. A., and Feldhamer, G. A., eds., 1982, *Wild Mammals of North America*: Johns Hopkins University Press.

Schmidt, C. A., 2003, "Conservation Assessment for the Small-Footed Myotis in the Black Hills National Forest, South Dakota, and Wyoming," Black Hills United States National Forest Assessment.

Shearwater Marketing Group online field guides website: www.enature.com

Snake River Birds of Prey National Conservation Area website: www.birdsofprey.blm.gov

Terres, J. K., 1995, *The Audubon Society Encyclopedia of North American Birds*: Wings Books (1st ed. 1980, Alfred A. Knopf).

Utah Division of Wildlife Resources website: http://wildlife.utah.gov

Whitaker, J. O., 1996, *National Audubon Society Field Guide to North American Mammals*: Alfred A. Knopf, Inc.

ARCHAEOLOGY AND HISTORY

Ashley National Forest website: http://www.fs.fed.us/r4/ashley/heritage (links to various topics from Paleoindians to recent history)

Castleton, K. B., M.D., 1984, *Petroglyphs and Pictographs of Utah, Vol. 1: The East and Northeast*: Utah Museum of Natural History.

———, 2002, *Petroglyphs and Pictographs of Utah, Vol. 2: The South, Central, West and Northwest*: Utah Museum of Natural History.

Cole, S. J., 1990, *Legacy on Stone: Rock Art of the Colorado Plateau and Four Corners Region*: Johnson Books.

Conetah, F. A., 1982, *History of the Northern Ute People*, Uintah–Ouray Ute Tribe.

Cuch, F. S. ed., 2004, *A History of Utah's American Indians*, Utah Division of Indian Affairs and Utah Historical Society.

Patterson, A., 1992, *Rock Art Symbols of the Greater Southwest*: Johnson Books.

Pettit, J., 1990, *Utes: The Mountain People*: Johnson Books.

Rockwell, W., 1998, *The Utes: A Forgotten People*: Western Reflections Publishing.

Smith, A. M., 1994, *Ethnography of the Northern Utes*: Museum of New Mexico Press.

Talbot, R. K., and Richens, L. D., 1997, *Steinaker Gap: An Early Fremont Farmstead*: University of Utah Press.

INDEX

GEOLOGY, PALEONTOLOGY, AND LANDSCAPE FEATURES

AUTHOR BIOGRAPHIES

MARY BETH BENNIS-SMITH

Mary Beth Bennis-Smith knew early on that the life of a naturalist was her calling. She began studying plants, wildlife, and geology long before she went through formal training. Mary Beth attended Colorado State University, where she majored in outdoor recreation, specializing as an interpreter. She also received her certification as a riding instructor.

After college, she went to work for Colorado State Parks, working as both a seasonal law enforcement ranger and interpretive supervisor. She was later hired on as a permanent park ranger with the state of Utah and received her Category I Peace Officer certification from P.O.S.T. (Peace Officer Standards and Training).

For seven years, she worked for Dinosaur National Monument as a quarry interpreter. During this time, she presented hundreds of talks on subjects ranging from dinosaurs to native plants. Mary Beth now works full-time for the Utah Field House of Natural History as the education curator where she has completed two museum guides for children.

Additionally, she has worked for both the Ashley and Dixie National Forests as a biological technician on Goshawk and endangered plant studies.

Her hobbies include horseback riding, reading, singing, running, and skiing.

DOUGLAS A. SPRINKEL

Doug Sprinkel is a senior geologist within the Geologic Mapping Program at the Utah Geological Survey. His principal responsibility is to conduct geologic mapping. His current mapping area includes the Uinta Basin and Uinta Mountains. Other research interests include a study of Early and Middle Jurassic rocks and unconformities. Doug has co-edited two popular books on Utah geology and authored or co-authored six geologic maps, fifty-four professional articles, and twenty-five abstracts.

Doug grew up in the Los Angeles, California, metropolitan area and attended college in southern California and Utah. He received his Bachelor of Science degree in 1975 and a Master of Science degree in 1977, both in geology, from Utah State University. During his thirty-one-year career, Doug has worked as an exploration geologist and district exploration manager for Placid Oil Company, working the Rocky Mountain and Great Basin areas, as well as in Canada, Mexico, and Turkey. After joining the Utah Geological Survey in 1986, Doug served as deputy director and research scientist in the Energy and Minerals Program before joining the Geologic Mapping Program. He has received several awards for his work at the Utah Geological Survey, including organization's highest, the Crawford Award.

LINDA WEST

During her twenty-year career in the National Park Service, Linda West has explained the mysteries of geology and paleontology to many a visitor. As a ranger-naturalist, she gave programs ranging from guided hikes among the spectacular cliffs of Capitol Reef National Park to "chalk talks" on dinosaurs at Dinosaur National Monument. She also wrote and illustrated several road and trail guides for both parks. She co-authored the trail guides *Dinosaur: The Dinosaur National Monument Quarry* and *Dinosaur: The Story Behind the Scenery*. Now semi-retired, Linda continues to put her interpretive and artistic talents to work as a volunteer. At the Utah Field House of Natural History State Park Museum, she repainted several of the Dinosaur Gardens models, illustrated a museum guidebook for youngsters, and helps present programs for visiting school groups. Most recently, she has given talks on geology and fossils for Ashley National Forest at the Red Canyon Visitor Center. Her current passion is photographing birds and other wildlife of the Uinta Mountains and Basin.

TOM ELDER

Tom Elder was born in Wichita, Kansas, in 1955, and grew up in the same town. In his youth, he spent a great deal of time on a cattle ranch in the Kansas Flint Hills, which gave him a lifelong taste for natural beauty and living things. He has a Bachelor of Science degree in wild land recreation management with an interpretation option from the University of Idaho's College of Forestry, Wildlife and Range. His first career was with the U.S. Forest Service and National Park Service working a variety of jobs, such as timber cruiser, wild land firefighter, wilderness ranger, and interpretive ranger. His jobs were at some of the West's "garden spots," such as Sawtooth National Recreation Area, Big Bend National Park, Grand Canyon National Park, Death Valley National Park, Black Canyon of the Gunnison National Monument and Dinosaur National Monument. He is married to Ann Elder, the curator at Dinosaur National Monument.

His second career is as a biology and anatomy teacher at Uintah High School in Vernal, Utah. He has spent nineteen years teaching, and enjoys exploring the wilds of Utah in his personal time.

NANCY BOSTICK-EBBERT

Nancy Bostick-Ebbert was born in Vernal, Utah, and grew up in the town of Bonanza. This talented author, artist, musician, and singer has two grown children and is married to a physician with Indian Health Services.

Some of her other accomplishments include:

Vernal Express, feature editor
Freelance Magazine, writer/photographer
SkyWest Magazine
Adventure Utah
Utah Highways
Numerous equine publications
Utah Statewide Archaeological News, editor
Conservation activist/writer
Singer/songwriter
Ute Creation Stories, soundtrack music
White River Video

RON STEWART

Ron Stewart has been working as the Conservation Outreach manager for the Northeastern Region of the Utah Division of Wildlife Resources for twenty years. Prior to getting a Master of Science degree in communication from Utah State, he worked for two years as a Peace Corps volunteer as a fisheries manager for the Kenyan government. He studied and photographed ospreys at Flaming Gorge to create a multi-projector slideshow for his Master's degree. Ron helped develop and write the original proposal for Highways 191 and 44 to become a State Scenic byway and the Flaming Gorge-Uintas National Scenic Byway. Since its acceptance, he has been the chairman of the Byway's Interpretive Committee and has provided text, photography, and many of the ideas for the interpretive signing, brochures, media coverage and magazine articles about the Byway. He considers *A Field Guide to the Flaming Gorge-Uintas National Scenic Byway* a major achievement, and has greatly enjoyed the opportunity to work with like-minded professionals to bring the incredible natural resources of the Byway to visitors' attention.